(continued from front flap)

we are going to have to do is restrain the faculty."

Nevitt Sanford writes, "Talent is often thought of in quantitative terms alone, rather than in human terms . . . as a high degree of mathematical ability, or a high test score. . . . I submit that [we] should consider the peaks of talent that may exist irrespective of test scores, irrespective of special attributes that might have been viewed narrowly as talent."

Ralph W. Tyler writes, "Educational opportunities [for minority students] are meaningless if those who are educated are not able to employ their talents in the society of which they are a part."

These are just a few highlights from *Issues of the Seventies,* a new book which sees many recent problems facing college administrators as important guideposts for the development of higher education in the new decade upon us. *Issues of the Seventies* presents a collection of original essays organized around three basic questions about higher education in the new decade: *What are society's concerns? What are the needs of students? What should colleges and universities do to answer these needs?* The authors approach these questions from many diverse points of view, often in conflict with each other. Each essay is followed by commentary—on-the-spot reactions to and criticisms of the arguments.

THE EDITOR

FRED F. HARCLEROAD is president of The American College Testing Program. The authors and their affiliations are listed in the front of the book.

ISSUES
OF THE
SEVENTIES

The Future
of
Higher Education

Edited by

Fred F. Harcleroad

issues of the seven- ties

 Jossey-Bass Inc., Publishers
615 Montgomery Street · San Francisco · 1970

ISSUES OF THE SEVENTIES
The Future of Higher Education
Fred F. Harcleroad, Editor

**Copyright © 1970 by American College Testing Program
Jossey-Bass, Inc., Publishers**

Jossey-Bass, Inc., Publishers
615 Montgomery Street
San Francisco, California 94111

Library of Congress Catalog Card Number 79–110639

Standard Book Number SBN 87589–057–1

Manufactured in the United States of America
    Composed and printed by York Composition Company, Inc.
    Bound by Chas. H. Bohn & Co., Inc.

JACKET DESIGN BY WILLI BAUM, SAN FRANCISCO

FIRST EDITION

Code 7008

THE JOSSEY-BASS SERIES IN HIGHER EDUCATION

General Editors

JOSEPH AXELROD
San Francisco State College

MERVIN B. FREEDMAN
*San Francisco State College and
Wright Institute, Berkeley*

Preface

The decade of the 1970s portends both promise and trial for American higher education. As a people, we must make a number of critical decisions in order to give our hopes and expectations every opportunity to come true. In the following chapters a diverse group of concerned spokesmen present their views on the critical areas for decision during the decade of the seventies. The topics revolve around three questions which are of fundamental importance to higher education: What are society's concerns? What are students' needs? And how should colleges and universities meet these often conflicting demands? These spokesmen address such problems as universal higher education, equal access to higher education, financial aid to college students, campus governance and power, the relationship of various campus groups, learning technology and the improvement of the instruction, and the urban crisis and its impact upon higher education.

These chapters were first presented as papers at the educational conference of the American College Testing Program, in May of 1969, to commemorate its first decade of service to students and higher education institutions. In 1976, this nation will celebrate two hundred years since it declared its independence and, in terms of

Preface

continuity, will be one of the oldest existing governments of our world. In order to last this long, our society has been extremely flexible and has adapted to the enormous changes which have taken place in the past twenty decades. We hope that these thoughtful essays, sometimes quite divergent in their approach to comparable problems, will contribute in a positive and helpful way to the continuing discussion which is necessary for our society to continue to adapt successfully and to move onward into its third century as a truly free and revolutionary society.

FRED F. HARCLEROAD

Iowa City, Iowa
February 1970

Contents

Contents

Contributors

AUTHORS

DAVID P. CAMPBELL, professor of psychology and assistant director of the Student Counseling Bureau, University of Minnesota

WILLIS E. DUGAN, executive director, American Personnel and Guidance Association

FRED F. HARCLEROAD, president, American College Testing Program

ROBERT HEINICH, professor of education, Indiana University

MAX LERNER, professor of American civilization and institutions, Brandeis University

JAMES A. MC CAIN, president, Kansas State University

THEODORE M. NELSON, dean of psychological services, Colorado State College

ROBERT S. POWELL, JR., president, United States National Student Association

DANIEL D. ROBINSON, partner, Peat, Marwick, Mitchell and Company, New York

Contributors

NEVITT SANFORD, director, Wright Institute, Berkeley

HAROLD TAYLOR, former president, Sarah Lawrence College

RALPH W. TYLER, director emeritus, Center for Advanced Study in the Behavioral Sciences

O. MEREDITH WILSON, director, Center for Advanced Study in the Behavioral Sciences

COMMENTATORS

LEONARD L. BAIRD, research psychologist, American College Testing Program

H. KENNETH BARKER, dean, College of Education, University of Akron

ELIAS BLAKE, JR., director of evaluation, Institute for Services to Education

JOSEPH D. BOYD, executive director, Illinois State Scholarship Program

LEE W. COCHRAN, director, Audiovisual Center, University of Iowa

JOHN J. COFFELT, vice-president, administrative affairs, Youngstown State University

NANCY S. COLE, research psychologist, American College Testing Program

DAVID S. CROCKETT, executive associate, American College Testing Program

OLUF M. DAVIDSEN, vice-president, program operations, American College Testing Program

LYLE D. EDMISON, dean of students, California State College at Hayward

ROBERT L. EWIGLEBEN, president, College of San Mateo

O. W. HASCALL, regional director, American College Testing Program

LOWELL HEINY, vice-president, Mesa College

DONALD P. HOYT, director of educational research, Kansas State University

Contributors

PHILLIP G. HUBBARD, dean of academic affairs, University of Iowa

PAUL F. LAWRENCE, San Francisco regional assistant commissioner, United States Office of Education

LEO A. MUNDAY, director, Research Services, American College Testing Program

ALLAN W. OSTAR, executive director, American Association of State Colleges and Universities

TED R. ROBINSON, director of admissions, Ohio State University

TOM G. SEXTON, director of higher education, Region VI, United States Office of Education

ARTHUR E. SMITH, vice-president, educational services, American College Testing Program

ROBERT C. SNIDER, associate executive secretary, Department of Audiovisual Instruction, National Education Association

RONALD B. THOMPSON, executive dean, Ohio State University

CARL VARNER, president, Associated Students, University of Iowa

CARL B. WIEMANN, JR., assistant to the president, American College Testing Program

ISSUES
OF THE
SEVENTIES

The Future
of
Higher Education

Fred F. Harcleroad

Issues of the Seventies

Prologue

As each decade fades into history the coming decade appears to be a time of hope and challenge, when past problems can be transformed into stepping stones for a more productive future. This can still be true of the decade of the seventies, in spite of the fact that college students of the sixties decided that the American dream had become a nightmare. In spite of the highest gross national product and the greatest material wealth per person ever achieved by any nation, the deficiencies which still exist in achieving the

1

goals of our Bill of Rights make it seem hollow to many college students. Thus we enter the 1970s with more questions than we had a decade earlier. New and seemingly more serious problems in higher education can and must be faced realistically during these important years just ahead.

However, the base on which to build has several strengths and provides good reason for some optimism. In order to view current problems of higher education in perspective, we can compare the situation at the end of World War II with that of today, a quarter of a century later. In 1945, the nation had 1,700 colleges and universities waiting for the veterans who would be returning from World War II. Many of these institutions had used up practically all of their reserves in order to keep going during the war. A number had closed but were hoping to be able to reopen. Only a million and a half students could be accommodated and it was correctly estimated that by the middle of the 1950s there would be three million students in higher education institutions.

Many educators had been concerned that the United States, dependent on private institutions which could not readily expand, would not have space for all the students who would need and demand admittance. However, the community colleges, the regional state colleges, and the state universities expanded rapidly and made provisions for the students. Now, entering the 1970s, we have 2,400 institutions of higher education and have doubled, again, in enrollment to six million students in those institutions. With the enormous increases in community colleges and regional state colleges and universities in the 1960s, a higher and higher percentage of the students graduating from high school can find a spot available if they have the interest and motivation to attend. States, private donors, and the federal government, with its enormous taxing power, have all increased their support of higher education. The achievement of universal higher education appears to be practically upon us.

Difficult days, however, clearly lie ahead; the expansion of the sixties has given rise, at least in part, to the problems we must face in the seventies. Undergraduate education has taken a back seat

2

Fred F. Harcleroad

while the graduate school and research subsidies have taken from teaching the attention of many of the finest faculty members. During this same period the problems of our central cities have become even more critical. It does not help that a high proportion of our higher education institutions are in rural areas with environments far different from those familiar to the increasing number of college students coming from the core areas of the central cities.

Our students, raised in comparative affluence in many cases, need not concern themselves primarily with earning the necessities of life but are greatly concerned that the constitutional guarantees of equal opportunity for all should be achieved, not just in their lifetime but instantly, in the very near future. This generation has determined to solve the problems inherent in the struggle for civil rights for all Americans. And they feel that the colleges and universities should be in the forefront of the struggle to provide full equality before the law for all citizens.

Kermit Gordon, President of the Brookings Institution, has pointed out (1968) that the central paradox of American society in 1968 was:

> On the one hand, we are a nation which sees itself as racked and divided over problems of poverty, riots, race, slums, unemployment, and crime. On the other hand, we are a nation which is clearly enjoying high prosperity, rapid economic growth, and a steady diffusion of affluence at a rate almost unimaginable a decade ago. [Although the economic goals of the sixties, steady prosperity and faster growth, have been achieved,] yet, today, the mood of the nation is more troubled, and our internal problems seem more stubborn and incurable, than was the case a decade ago.

It is in this context that Harold Taylor emphasizes in his chapter the importance of rapid development of our communication systems in changing our way of life:

> Before the eyes of the younger generation, the inequities and injustices of the American community were revealed by the public media of television, the news magazines, and the paperbacks. . . . In the latter years of the 1950s, a new generation of young people came alive to the realities of social injustice

3

in America by seeing before their eyes members of their own
generation beaten by police, goaded by cattle prods, brutalized
by attackers, jailed, and in some cases killed. This was advertised to us in national reports on television and in the mass
media. In that point in time, a new attitude was generated
within the younger generation and became part of contemporary history. A new generation, having been subsidized by
the educational system and informed by the mass media about
the reality of contemporary society, moved into an era in
which many of the young knew more about their own society
than did their elders.

The students whom he describes are of the generation who entered
the colleges and universities during the last half of the 1960s and
who prepared the way for the problem areas and major changes of
the 1970s.

The chapters of Part One explore, as the title reveals,
society's concerns. O. Meredith Wilson stresses, as a first priority,
a need to make our higher educational institutions credible within
the ethical boundaries of our Constitution. With the Vietnam war
a chief cause of concern and unease in our society, he points out
the incongruity of colleges and universities as "shelters from the
draft" rather than as places in which students can develop and
use their minds. And, simultaneously, only a restricted group of
persons can secure the right to attend and achieve a "haven."
Wilson also concerns himself with the other raw and open sore of
our society: the unequal opportunity for black people and other
minority groups. Our climate of racism does not permit our
minorities to enroll in college and achieve the current and future
advantages that accrue from attending a college or university. Max
Lerner concerns himself with some of the same questions and, in
particular, the crisis in the cities. Describing the United States as
"one of the most revolutionary societies in the world today," he
believes that the "authenticity and validity of the American dream"
can be restored as we provide for every citizen "a sense of himself
as a person," and recognize "his identity and worth, his dignity
and pride." Lerner also stressed the impact of television and its
effect on the ideas and desires of all of our disadvantaged minorities.

Lerner emphasizes the problem of "instantism," in which everything presented on television is something which is available instantly. He indicates that the most important thing in democracy is "access"—first to income, which comes by getting jobs and skills; second, to power, which helps control what is happening around a person; third, to education, in order to prepare themselves for future opportunities; and finally, fourth, to a sense of identity. If higher education in the seventies can provide these four things for our minority groups, or assist them in working toward them, it should help to restore some part of the eroded American dream.

The essays by Dugan and Sanford stress, respectively, the importance of truly equal opportunity for access to higher education and the problems in the loss of talent if equal opportunity is not available. Sanford differentiates between the loss of talent as an economic problem of needed manpower and as a human problem of a social nature. Sanford emphasizes the need for diversity in undergraduate institutions in the United States in order that all types of talent can be sought out and provided with an opportunity to blossom. He also pressed the need for teachers, rather than researchers, to serve the students in the undergraduate colleges. In the comments after his speech he emphasized his hopes that "this current generation of students will produce a whole new population of teachers" of a type which will spend their time with future generations of students. Allan Ostar, Executive Director of the American Association of State Colleges and Universities, commented in discussion after Dugan's speech that the "research evidence [is] available that we have a better chance for students . . . when there are institutions available that have flexible admission policies and relatively low tuition charges" rather than simply having institutions with large financial aid programs. He graphically compared California and New Jersey as extreme examples, since California has 80 per cent or more of all high school graduates going on to some kind of post-secondary higher education and New Jersey has only 30 per cent of high school graduates going on to comparable post-secondary education. He wonders, and well he might, whether much of this is because California students coming into high school know that there is an institution somewhere in the state to which they can go and which they can afford. In New Jersey, on the other hand, the expectation of high school graduates is relatively low because of the limited amount of educational opportunity available in terms of both cost and the number of spaces available. Wilson earlier made this same point, in connection with the education of black students, emphasizing the importance of the expectation of the individual as a factor in his going on to college and being successful in his work there.

Part Two of this book is concerned with student needs. Robert S. Powell, Jr., President of the National Student Association in 1968–69, dramatically emphasizes what seems to be more and more true to more and more students—namely, that their true enemy is the organized faculty. Powell points out that persuasion has seldom worked in recent university confrontations and that violence has often led to rapid change. Although he neither espouses violence nor condones it, he makes the point that students realize that violence seems to be successful if they pursue it seriously enough. He hopes that the rule of reason will prevail, rather than the rule of force; but he does feel that definite brakes must be placed on the power of the faculty and increased rights must be given to organized students in the governance of the college campus.

Both Powell and Taylor emphasize the need for students to be fully accepted as equal voting partners in the development of curricula, and in the selection, retention, and promotion of faculty. Powell states that only through such revolutionary changes will student problems of the sixties be resolved in the seventies and provide the independent citizens, thinking for themselves, who are needed for a free democracy.

On another tack, David Campbell and Theodore Nelson point up the importance of accurate assessment instruments, relatively open admissions, and well-organized and well-conducted guidance services, in order that students can be provided with an optimum opportunity for success in their higher educational career. Campbell describes the major changes that take place in an institution when its student body is changed dramatically over a period

6

of years by use of differing admissions procedures. And once again, both contributors stress the need for diversity in our institutions in order to serve diverse faculty and diverse students. They also suggest that the success of an institution might be judged better by the number of students who are successful in completing the program of the college than by maintaining high attrition rates. Expanded guidance and psychological services for students will be necessary in order to achieve such results, and not necessarily limited only to special services for minority or disadvantaged students.

Part Three, "Institutional Response," addresses the question, what should the colleges do in order to meet the needs of students and provide for the concerns of our society?

In analyzing and prescribing for current campus unrest, James McCain points out some of the reasons for student unrest and two indispensable institutional assets which are endangered by the unrest—the need for public confidence and support, and the need for the academic community to have freedom to manage its own affairs. Although students have found that "violence gets results," President McCain emphasizes that these results may have been purchased at a very dear price and that public support may have been seriously disturbed. Daniel Robinson, reflecting on unrest as a mirror of society's deep-seated uneasiness and the problem of technology as it moves too fast for the society it is intended to serve, suggests some concrete measures that college management personnel can take to make better use of the resources currently available. He suggests the need for jointly developed organizational structure, well-planned budgets and operational controls, management information systems and carefully developed operating systems. In considering changes in academic governance these four areas need clear delineation along with the consideration by the various campus groups which must be involved in the campus governance and operation. Clearly defined purposes, agreed upon by the various campus publics, can provide not only for optimum use of funds but for a lessening of campus tension.

Robert Heinich, in his discussion of technology and the student, addresses himself to improving teaching, one of the most

7

recurrent problems brought up by students. They are quite concerned about the lack of attention to teaching as a function on the campus and the development of impersonalism and researchism in place of the teaching emphasis. At the same time students cry out against the impersonalism which is a possible result of technology. Heinich points out the sophistication of modern students in the use of today's media. Students deal daily with the mass media and take for granted the instant availability of news from all over the world. They also are quite willing to use any of the advantages of modern technology in carrying out any protest activities. As Heinich says, "The young do not reject technology, they do reject mechanization." Heinich specializes in the use of media as assistance to students in learning and to assist professors in providing instruction. And he concludes, "The student must stop having to shed the twentieth century when he enters the college classroom."

Finally, in the Epilogue, Ralph Tyler addresses himself to one of the key questions of our time, "Are academic excellence and equal opportunity compatible?" After reviewing the impact of social changes on American education and seven conditions that are essential on the campus for students to learn complex and difficult things, Tyler concludes that American higher educational institutions "can effectively help in the education of a much larger proportion of youth than is now being reached while at the same time their academic excellence can be greatly increased."

The chapters that follow are a mirror of a disturbed, agitated, and sometimes violent period of higher education. The decade of the seventies will certainly contain more of the same. Students, having tasted a sense of freedom and power, will continue to insist on treatment as adults. They can be expected to push harder and harder for the improvement of teaching and for the personalization of the academic process for undergraduates. They have experienced success in breaking down the in loco parentis approach to campus living and are anticipating a greater and greater say in the actual academic governance of the campus. Both the students and the lay public appear to be focusing in on the faculty as the central cause of campus problems. With faculties basically

Fred F. Harcleroad

in control of campus governance to a greater degree than ever before in the history of higher education, the struggle for power will be vigorous and constant. Higher education has never been as well off as it is today. Neither has the society it serves. It remains to be seen whether the diverse groups on various campuses can resolve their differences—or whether, in fact, the off-campus stresses and strains will allow any peace on the campus. Certainly, free open discussion of the issues is the first necessary step. And these chapters, representing wide differences of opinion, are a small contribution to the essential dialogue.

PART ONE

SOCIETY'S
CONCERNS

O. Meredith Wilson

Our First Priority: A Credible Ethic

1

Much of the unrest and anxiety that our society suffers on the university campus is the consequence of defects that are not clearly located. A fair hypothesis is that the defects may be defects of our society and that the people of the appropriate age to feel those defects find in the university their place of congregation. A university is an institution which, to perform its role satisfactorily, needs to live somewhat apart from society; to be really relevant to the sense of competence to perform its chores, it needs some social

13

distance. Therefore I quote with affirmation the observation of Lord Bryce, "A university should be concerned with its times but should not give in to them." I believe that the defects are essentially in our whole society, so the question under discussion is not so much what our universities should do as it is what *we* should do.

The question is, are our priorities mixed up? First we must determine of whom we speak when we ask the question. The country at large? If so, then is the first priority peace, or simply peace in Vietnam? And if it is peace of either kind, is it because its priority is dictated by the human spirit, or by ethical considerations, or by fear? Or, is it because our economy can no longer bear the burden? Is peace merely a means of stopping inflation?

Is it justice and equal opportunity for all that require our first attention? Or is it order? Will violence authored by men who suffer injustice lead men who value order to destroy freedom? Can there be any value in an order that permits, disguises, or even condones injustice? Can there be real peace, real order, authentic public weal if some men are denied full civic participation; if those men are afforded employment beneath their preparation, and preparation beneath their potential? Can it be, after all, that the first item on the agenda for the nation is still to make credible the first canon among the principles that fired the imagination of our founding fathers?

> We hold these truths to be self evident: that all men are created equal; that they are endowed by their Creator with certain unalienable rights; that among these are life, liberty, and the pursuit of happiness.

In Jefferson's mind it was to secure these rights that governments were instituted among men. If their enjoyment is still wanting among substantial numbers of our people, then winning those rights for all men must remain the first objective of government.

How do unalienable rights relate to peace in Vietnam? A conscript war is fought by career officers, either from the academies or the ROTC's, and by men who have no shelter from conscription. Look at our society and ask who are most exposed? They appear

14

to me to be young men of eighteen to twenty-six, who for some reason are not enrolled, or do not remain enrolled, in colleges or universities, and who thus have no access to a II-S classification. Or they may be volunteers, to whom defense enlistment is an opportunity—perhaps their only opportunity—for upward mobility. It may not be too much to ask: Are those who are given least opportunity in civilian life given the greatest chance to die for their country? Are they led to believe that by gambling their lives in war they may find a better career which is otherwise closed to them?

If being either in school or out of school at age twenty can make the difference between fighting and not fighting in a war that awakens few moral convictions, then is not our first priority to insure an even-handed distribution of the opportunities to be in school? But surely we cannot have created schools for so strange a purpose. They were not established as shelters from the draft, and equal access to them cannot be defended only because we wish to make more equal the burdens of a war. The reason the student is granted a deferment is that our countrymen believe that human beings are our greatest national assets, and that education is a means by which we can greatly enhance those assets. The student, being educated, is more valuable to the nation. He is also better for himself, for his family; he is more fully a man and more likely to be able to earn a good living and live a good life. So, the young man who would like to be, but cannot be, in college at age twenty is not only in greater peril for his life, but, if he lives, has a lesser chance for preparation for a rewarding future. How can he believe he is protected in those "unalienable rights"?

Now we ask further: Of whose priorities do we speak? Of the priorities of educational institutions? How shall we determine who shall be admitted? How shall they be educated? Shall we honor Thoreau and allow—perhaps even encourage—some to march to different drummers? Can there be a cacophony of drums and rhythms, or do we need a common marching step to insure to us, since we have a common destination, a shared progression? The lines of a poem written by a loyalist during the Spanish Civil War come to mind, but I have revised them to sustain the mood of inquiry:

> Is the idea to get there first and alone
> Or with all and on time?

There are also priorities of educational values. Are our needs to be satisfied merely by more know-how, or do we require some know-why as well? Has religious underpinning been so shaken that no purpose in life can be defended until a differently based and credible ethic can be discovered and win common acceptance?

How does this question of priorities affect college testing programs? Shall we be content to continue sorting young men and women, putting some in a bin from which top colleges may draw, others into a more general grab bag, still others into the pool for draftees? Or can we address ourselves, rather, to more fundamental problems? Can we design tests that will be diagnostic, and thus help make methods of instruction more precise? Can we be creative forces toward building men instead of being content to sort them as we find them?

One of the grave problems of the hour arises from the widespread belief that educational institutions are central to the shaping of modern men and the bitter recognition that only some men are being served by them. And it is no comfort to repeat the scriptural pronouncement: "To them that have shall be given." Men and women now old enough to go to college, and by traditional standards not adequately prepared, are not content to live all their lives without opportunity while we try to prevent their younger brothers and sisters from being similarly deprived through the efforts of Head Start, or Better Chance, or Teachers' Corps.

A board, a committee, or any convened body of scholars is apt to conceive of itself as a task force called into being to redress the most obvious grievance. And any discussion of priorities is likely to focus on the current shortcomings, not on extrapolated or more far-reaching exigencies. As a result the product of most such meetings is an ad hoc decision committing a major part of the available creative energy to a new priority program.

In the early 1950s a national anxiety was aroused by the discovery that we were wasting our most promising resources. Half of our top 25 percentile students in high school were not going on to college. College testers revealed the tragedy, but were somewhat slow to explain that a disproportionate number of top achievers in high school were girls, who were less likely than boys to continue their education. At that time a first priority might have developed around equal rights, equal opportunities, and equal pay for women; but before a full head of protest could be built up, a new threat to excellence was unmasked. The last two years of high school seemed to leave the bright student untested, and the first two years of college repeated what he had already learned. Society thereupon committed itself to creating the circumstances in which the best minds could be encouraged, stretched, paced, and even prodded. Tests to sort the types were invoked; curricular committees were convened; and advanced placement and early admissions programs blossomed across the landscape. Educational activists had set as first priority the scrapping of the procrustean beds in educational institutions. By better articulation institutions were to respond to the needs and capabilities of each person rather than force all students to adjust to the established institutional dimensions. Good students were going to be encouraged into excellence by tender loving and personalized care.

This account may sound ironic, but I am convinced that the excellence phase had value. It was interrupted or overshadowed, though not deliberately discarded, as Sputnik focused our attention on the sciences, and aroused our concern for the progress of a special segment of the gifted.

Now we are beset with a more thorny bramble of questions. How troubled are we to learn that blacks, who constitute 11 per cent of our total population, provide only 4.5 per cent of our college enrollment, and less than 1.0 per cent of our professional and doctoral degree holders? How much do we know about the

effects of expectation on progress? Do you share my intuitive judgment that the four-minute mile became easier for athletes everywhere once Roger Bannister had proved it to be possible? Or that
children encouraged to believe they can meet an assignment are
more likely to fulfill it than are children who believe that we doubt
them? What are the consequences of social expectation on a class
of people who have learned from experience that they are branded
as impertinent if they perform above their station? Finally, what
effect on effort should be expected from a continuous record of
vocational placements below comparable placements of men of
equal preparation? Would the consequences of underexpectation,
undereducation, and underplacement be similar whatever the race?
Should we not expect such underranked people to ask, "Why
should I strive by special grace when the way of the world is
closed to me?" This is a quotation from W. E. B. DuBois and it
leads me to a longer quotation from him, a quotation that, although
it does not respond to each of these questions, seems worth our
attention:

> The worlds within and without the Veil of Color are changing,
> and changing rapidly, but not at the same rate, not in the
> same way; and this must produce a peculiar wrenching of the
> soul, a peculiar sense of doubt and bewilderment. Such a dou-
> ble life, with double thoughts, double duties, and double social
> classes, must give rise to double words and double ideals, and
> tempt the mind to pretence or revolt, to hypocrisy or radical-
> ism.
>
> In some such doubtful words and phrases can one perhaps
> most clearly picture the peculiar ethical paradox that faces
> the Negro of today and is tingeing and changing his religious
> life. . . . Conscious of his impotence, and pessimistic, he
> often becomes bitter and vindictive; and his religion, instead
> of a worship, is a complaint and a curse, a wail rather than a
> hope, a sneer rather than a faith. On the other hand, another
> type of mind, shrewder and keener and more tortuous too,
> sees in the very strength of the anti-Negro movement its patent
> weaknesses, and with Jesuitic casuistry is deterred by no ethical
> considerations in the endeavor to turn this weakness to the
> black man's strength. Thus we have two great and hardly

reconcilable streams of thought and ethical striving; the danger of the one lies in anarchy, that of the other in hypocrisy.

Deception is the natural defense of the weak against the strong, and the South used it for many years against its conquerors. Today it must be prepared to see its black proletariate turn that same two-edged weapon against itself. And how natural this is! The death of Denmark Vesey and Nat Turner proved long since to the Negro the present hopelessness of physical defense. Political defense is becoming less and less available, and economic defense is still only partially effective. But there is a patent defense at hand,—the defense of deception and flattery, of cajoling and lying. It is the same defense which peasants of the Middle Age used and which left its stamp on their character for centuries. Today the young Negro of the South who would succeed cannot be frank and outspoken, honest and self-assertive, but rather he is daily tempted to be silent and wary, politic and sly; he must flatter and be pleasant, endure petty insults with a smile, shut his eyes to the wrong; in too many cases he sees positive personal advantage in deception and lying. His real thoughts, his real aspirations, must be guarded in whispers. He must not criticise. He must not complain. Patience, humility, and adroitness must in these growing black youth, replace impulse, manliness, and courage. With this sacrifice there is an economic opening, and perhaps peace and some prosperity. Without this there is riot, migration, or crime. Nor is this situation peculiar to the Southern United States; is it not rather the only method by which undeveloped races have gained the right to share modern culture? The price of culture is a lie [1961].

You may choose for yourself your own reaction to DuBois. But if the refractions or the distortions of character which he alleges as being an inevitable consequence of being treated as less than a full member of the community are in any sense true, some revolution against and emergence from cowering into manliness is a social good.

In our design of tests that are intended primarily to sort, a decent respect for the minds of men should make us meticulously careful to avoid not only channeling blacksmiths to scholarship, but, much worse, diverting potential scholars to blacksmithing, because we would thereby foreclose to someone the development and use of his mind, the vocation among all vocations most singularly human. In addition we should search for instruments that might diagnose causes of poor performance and permit corrective prescriptions, so that each man might have available to him the education best suited to his self-fulfillment.

A review of our shifting priorities should not lead us to believe we were once concerned about excellence but no longer; nor that we were once enlisted to prevent wasting time in preparatory school, and duplication and boredom in the early years of college, but now are not; nor that the gifted science student was once a special concern but must now take a back seat because we have time only for the disadvantaged. We must have time for them all, because they are all mankind, all capable of dignity but each still short of self-fulfillment. And, with that summary, our persisting priority is uncovered. It is the cultivation and the perfection of individual men. No mass formula will serve them all, because there is no education for the masses. Masses are swayed; individuals are educated. And to be educated properly their individuality must be respected. The gifted, the scientist, the generalist, the disadvantaged all have their distinctive needs, including a gait, a pace, a rhythm appropriate to their own abilities and background. Each deserves as much attention, as much education as will help him (and as much as he is willing to use) in his private-public struggle to perfect his talents.

Out of a rich heritage of social documents that include the Declaration of Independence, the Federalist Papers, the Constitution, the Bill of Rights, the decisions of Marshall, the speeches, letters, and papers of Lincoln, our people have struggled to cultivate an ethos for this nation. Unfortunately, the growth upward and outward from a slave-holding, Indian-fighting, sin-hating Protestant parochialism has been very slow. We do not really need a new ethic; we need only to make credible the ethic expressed in the Declaration of Independence. We will not have a credible ethic as long as we lack an authentic ethos. The raw material for such an ethos is at hand. I covet for us, now, not postponed for later

20

generations, a public performance that can ease our troubled national conscience and make it possible for our idealistic young to speak of our land as the land of the free, not with a grimace of doubt but with a smile of affirmation. If without a regeneration of faith in God and restoration of concern for the soul, then through a respect for our fellow men, a respect for national integrity, through reasoned judgment as to the rightness of things, we must by our behavior make real our ethos and credible our national ethic.

Commentary

O. Meredith Wilson

In the first of the magnificent Federalist Papers Alexander Hamilton, who was still quite young, wrote that it seemed to be reserved to people of his generation to determine once and for all whether it could be possible that governments of men can be determined by reason and choice or whether we must always depend on accident and force. I believe that they made a major stride toward establishing the fact that reason and choice could be the instruments of men. My own reading of history is that, in spite of our present shortcomings, we stand on a plateau substantially higher in our respect for men generally than we did at that time, in part because of the guides they gave us on how to proceed.

I do not know of any shortcut to creation of perfection. I do not know any other way to achieve the fullest stature of humanity than to become reasonable and to respond honestly to the data before you with as much richness as the mind can bring to the problem. I do not know any instrument quite as good at the cultivation of reason. Educators who have been long in the business should, first, throw away the disposition toward impatience; second, reaffirm their judgment that we are essentially men of reason; and third, insist that violence is an interruption of reason which is catastrophic. We should try to find means to persuade the young that even we were once nineteen, and we have some advantage over them because, having been nineteen, we know more about where they are than they may know about where we are.

Ultimately, the present campus dissenters are our children. They are either our sons and daughters or our nieces and nephews and they arrive at the campus already prepared to protest. The university is more nearly the place where the disenchanted convene than it is the place where they are created. Their disenchantment is with imperfection, for probably nothing is clearer than the fact that the most troublesome thing is not a complete failure of moral ambition but a partially achieved goal. And it is in the presence of our partially achieved goals—and in the presence of our efforts to achieve those goals by admitting people who heretofore had been excluded from the campuses—that we have created problems that trouble us. I think accepting modesty, accepting a pace which is strong and affirmative but short of violence, rather than insisting upon overwhelming society by revolution, is the first step. There is no really fast way to perfect men. You have to educate every new generation freshly. The only real hope I have is that we will recognize reason as our fulfillment and use the university as a means to that end, and that, as nearly as possible, we will exclude force and violence. And so I refer you again to the first Federalist Paper.

I would like to sound a warning. We are disposed to accept very dogmatic statements from students that we would reject out of hand if they were made by a faculty. As a matter of fact, one of the most troublesome things in the present conversation between faculty and students is the disposition of the students to be so sure of themselves. One of the consequences of education, if it is good education, is some development of mellowing and modesty. One of the primary characteristics of the present clash of generations is

22

the disposition of young students to sound like students from the days of Oliver Cromwell. The emotional overtones to their statements are clearly parallel. In fact, it would be proper to say that the most difficult thing the university president or dean faces now is the bald, accusatory, sharp confrontation in which an opinion is a fact, and all of the world of adults is described as evil and all of the world of the young as good. Somehow pressed into the corner by a conspiring evil society, they are, as young people, the modern populists. One of the fascinating things is that they, like the elder populists, have arrived at a position from which they can command all other parts of our society to observe civic principles to which they are not obligated. Our society has developed a tradition of granting authority to the majority and guaranteeing the protection of the individual by a Bill of Rights. There used to be no protection for the individual once the will of the majority was determined. Indeed, from the history that I remember, this sort of arrogance of the majority led Athens to hand Socrates a cup of hemlock. There was no Bill of Rights to protect Socrates, so he drank it. The student populists, with their participatory democracy, begin with the ideas that the only demonstration of democracy is that each man participate in the sovereign judgment. I am of the judgment that there is danger in being too romantic about populist wisdom and goodness. They are still young and they are often not modest.

One of the chief errors of this generation flows from the belief that whenever there is a trouble or an awkwardness or a misfortune the appropriate solution is a new university course. The university has the obligation to deal with those problems that will respond to reason, search and inquiry, and the development of the mind. Literally dozens of things that are important to our society would be better prepared for outside the university. We now are victims of the university syndrome which leads us even when we establish a good pretechnical institute to want it to become a four-year school and then a four-year school plus graduate work, as though it is impossible to serve God or do any particular job unless you have over your building the imprimatur, *university*. One of our problems is to be more clear about both the great potential and the clear limitations of the university. Beyond that, then, there are still many differentiated functions that can be performed among universities. One of the great achievements of America has been the development of a pluralistic system of higher education, and I would consider it a tragedy if we arrived at a decision that every institution must somehow conform to Harvard's standard of admissions, grading, and graduation. I even consider it to be a major value in our society that people can emerge from very different kinds of universities with a bachelor's degree and feel that they can be free members of a competing society, unconcerned that they are bachelors from an institution at which graduation ends where admission begins elsewhere.

David S. Crockett

Who really sets the priorities in our society? Is it the majority? I think there is ample evidence in our society today that the majority is not always right. Yet, in a democracy we are somehow ingrained with the idea that the majority is right and certainly the question is, then, "Who does set the priorities?" And how can the majority be influenced if they are wrong? I think that is what students are really talking about today. How do you go about influencing the majority which you think is wrong and which may well be wrong? Certainly one way to do this is one that most people deplore, the use of violence, which has brought about a lot of very positive change in this country. Columbia is a good example. Columbia is a different place today than it was a year ago. There have been some changes. Our priorities do change and shift.

Paul F. Lawrence

The discussion inevitably gets around to student unrest on the campus. No other single issue in the history of education has generated so much interest and concern, not only among professional educators but among the general population. I must say also that no other issue defies explanation and analysis as much as the phenomenon of student unrest. I suppose you heard about the college president, just a year ago, asked to deliver a paper on the student life at his institution, who chose to direct his subject toward a rather smug analysis on why student unrest did not occur, could not occur, and would never occur, on his campus. Not more than half way through his speech, the president received a telephone call to come out because on his campus there was a major student demonstration. This is a fact, not an exaggeration.

I think it important for our purpose to establish where we are in our knowledge of student unrest. Then, we could find some of the goals for further consideration and research and establish what I would consider some real priorities. Generally, we know that students demonstrate in various ways to emphasize a point that they are trying to bring to the attention of the college officials. The form of demonstration varies considerably depending only on the limits of imagination of the students taking part in it. We are told that the object of these demonstrations is reform of curricula, of rules and regulations, of committee structure and composition, of all the ways that universities and colleges view their purposes and missions, and sometimes, unfortunately, reform of a university out of existence. It is obvious to most of us that although there will be acrimonious debate and grasping at outworn traditions, a reform will eventually change much of our college and university life. Students realize this too; it is only a matter of time for them. The question now is not whether, but when.

Max Lerner

Colleges and the Urban Crisis

2

I come to you from the wars, in a sense; we have a new kind of war correspondent these days. I was at Columbia last spring when that happened at Columbia. I was at Sorbonne soon after that, when it happened in Paris at the university there. I was in Chicago, at the Democratic national convention when the confrontation happened. I was at Cornell recently when that happened there. I was at Brandeis awhile before that when we had our episode. I was at CCNY. I am a war correspondent; I come to you from the wars. And as I have traveled around among these wars I have asked some questions, both of students and of administrators and faculty. Perhaps I can generalize a bit from what happened at Chicago. I was there as a columnist, and as a commentator, I thought I would try to make an estimate of what had happened. When I got back home I tried to catch up with some of the columns of my colleagues. As I read these columns about what had happened in Chicago, I rubbed my eyes in disbelief. This was not what I had seen. Almost every one of them—and these were my colleagues somewhere to the right of me, perhaps, if I may call it that—almost every one of them described the scene in the same way; that is, the way the young people looked—their abundance of hair, their side-burns, their beards, their messy clothes, their smell, their stench. I read these things and I said, "My God, they're looking at the whole thing through the eyes of a sanitation engineer!"

Now, I believe in public health, very much, and public hygiene; but I also believe in mental health, which I think may be perhaps more crucial. What I saw was rather different. What I saw was the hunger for power among those who felt themselves power-less to stop the war, and to end the draft; the hunger for participation, for decision-making among those who felt themselves left out. I went back to one of my culture heroes, Justice Holmes. He said a man must have a share in the passions and actions of his time, at the peril of being judged not to have lived. A hunger for partici-pation, a hunger for fellowship, a hunger for belief—these are the hungers I saw, and I saw them on both sides. I saw hungers among the Chicago police, too. Hunger to be considered a human being, hunger not to be called racist pig. As someone said, the best pig is a dead pig. Hunger not to be called a racist pig, a hunger for self-respect, or the crucial thing that a man carries around with him, his self-image. A hunger to be valued for the dangerous oc-cupation that he is pursuing. I saw hungers there, too. And, of course, neither side saw the hungers of the other and what resulted was polarization of hatreds, and the final result was what we saw— one of the tragic events of recent years.

Today is a time of testing—the testing of institutions and

leadership, testing to see whether our cities are viable, whether our colleges can really function, whether our democratic processes can contain the revolutionary changes that are taking place. As I have traveled around the world a bit, I have found some of my friends saying to me, "Mr. Lerner, this reactionary America of yours," and I say, "Wait a minute—if you mean you don't like some of the decisions of our leaders, that's your privilege, some of us don't. But if you mean that America is itself a reactionary society then watch out. It isn't so. It's probably the most revolutionary society in the world today." This always rocks them back on their heels—America revolutionary!

Then, of course, I have tried to point out there are two basic meanings of revolution. One is the classical historical meaning —overthrowing the regime, subverting the society by direct action of planned violence. The other, much more important, is an accelerated rate of change inside the society, without violence, at least with violence only very, very marginal. Without violence, a rate of change so rapid as to achieve a whole succession of breakthroughs. This gives new levels from which further changes take place.

Now, these changes in our society have been going on for some time; they preceded the college malaise, the college unrest, they preceded the war, they preceded the draft, they preceded all of that. And it is in this sense that America is the most revolutionary society in the world today, much more so than those that call themselves revolutionary—Communist Russia, China, Cuba. We are far more revolutionary, because in those countries when changes begin, they are not allowed to work themselves out. In our country, which is still a tolerably open society, they do work themselves out. They work themselves out all the way, and that is our concern, of course, now. We are trying to see how they will work themselves out. A little like that song, "June Is Busting Out All Over," America is busting out all over—bursting at the seams. We are a little like Pandora's box—box of the winds. The winds were let out and they can never be put back into the box. And the winds are out. The question is what do we do.

Max Lerner

I did a book on American civilization at the end of the 1950s (Lerner, 1957). I was describing changes that had been going on since the end of World War II. Obviously, if I were to do a revision, as I hope to do, I would point out that in the last ten years the changes have been even more rapid. America has been changing very rapidly, more rapidly than any other civilization in the world. The real question is whether we have been changing adequately, and in the right direction, and whether these changes will continue to take place inside society, within the basic structure of the linkage of human being with human being, revolutionary changes in the second sense of the term, or will spill over into the first sense, the planned violent subversion of a regime and of the whole society. I hope we will be hospitable to change. I hope also we will have the kind of collective will to contain these changes so that they take place within not only the rule of law, but the rule of ideas. There is no way of telling.

When people say to me, "Are you an optimist or a pessimist?" I say, "What do you think this is, Wall Street? Do you think this is a question of whether I am bullish or bearish about the gyrations of stocks on the stock market? I'm neither an optimist nor a pessimist; I am a possibilist. I think it's going to be possible to contain these changes. But that doesn't mean it's guaranteed. That depends on our collective intelligence and our collective will."

Peter Drucker has done a remarkable book (1968) on what he calls the "discontinuities" that are now going on in American society. *The Age of Discontinuity* he calls it. I suppose he means the same by *discontinuities* as I mean by *revolutionary changes* in this second sense of the term *revolution*. That is, when you look at our history you see, obviously, a line of continuity of change. But when the changes get very accelerated, and they escalate, then you get not so much continuity as discontinuity—a break in continuity. And these changes are now putting a strain on personality structure in the United States (the "American character") and on institutions and legal processes and codes.

This is pretty much what I want to discuss—not as some of our friends of the extreme right do, who set their faces stonily

29

against change of any kind, nor as some of my friends on the far-out left, who make a cult of violent change, and seem to get some kind of emotional charge by being some way associated with violence. They have a romantic feeling about violence, almost the sense that there is a purging effect in it. I do not go with that. I have read too much of history, I have seen too much of what violence has done to believe that there is any kind of purging, releasing impact to mass violence. And so I say the frame of these comments must be one of generosity toward change.

The main thrust of our recent changes, obviously, has been in the direction of an erosion of belief. I had a friend, Harold Laski, who was one of the important intellectual leaders of the British Labour Party. I remember his saying toward the end of World War II, "When the leaders of the people ask their followers to die for a dream, those followers have a right to know in whose behalf the dream is being dreamt." In every civilization worth anything, there is, at the very core, a dream. When we talk of the American dream, what do we mean? We mean a vision of social possibility, of how life can be lived on this continent. There has been continuity in that dream ever since the first American revolution, and the Jeffersonian revolution, and the Jacksonian, and all the rest right up to the present time. The real question is in whose behalf the dream is being dreamt. In two areas of our lives, in the inner-city ghettos and on college campuses today, this question is being asked in a mocking and derisive way. In the inner-city ghetto it is being asked by young people who come from underprivileged groups. It is being asked on college campuses mainly by the sons and daughters of privileged groups.

The fact that they are asking this question is an important fact, because it represents an erosion of belief in the authenticity and validity of the American dream. We are not going to be able to speak of social peace until we have recast that dream and made it credible. Which means, incidentally, making our civilization viable. As we look at the history of great civilizations that lived, prospered, flourished, and died, the lesson we can learn from them is not that we shall die from poverty or from too little power or from the thrust of barbarians outside our walls. Nothing like that. I think our great vulnerability comes within our walls, in terms of the erosion of belief. If we can make the dream credible, then I think we will have achieved something.

People say America is a sick society; I do not think it is. There are sick ideas in the society, and sick groups, but I do not think that in itself it is a sick society. I think it is a tragic society, tragically split. I take the meaning of tragedy from a German philosopher, Max Scheler. He did some essays on Greek tragedy in which he pointed out that the protagonists are not evil: they are men of high purpose aiming at very high goals, especially justice. But as they aim at these goals they come in conflict with the laws of the gods—life and society—and they destroy something more precious than that which they are pursuing.

That, to me, is the nature of the tragic experience as we are living it in our country today. I see very few evil men on either side of the barricades. I see men of high purpose within their own minds, seeking what seem to them to be lofty goals. But I also see these men in conflict with the laws of life of the society, which enable a society to survive. I see them destroying the fabric of the society itself. I find that particularly true on college campuses. America is today a split and wounded society; the question is how to heal those wounds. As a possibilist I think they can be healed, with time and intelligence and will. But it is not guaranteed.

Let me say a few words about the inner-city revolution. It is part of a much broader and deeper *uprooting revolution* that has been going on for some time. We are being uprooted from the farm, from the land, from the small town, from the city neighborhood, from religious institutions, from codes of sexual behavior, from esthetic codes. We are part of a deep uprooting, and the inner city is part of it. What we have now in the inner city is the product of two vast geographical movements which came pretty much at the same time, but were not necessarily related to each other. One was the movement by American Negroes out of the southern communities into the big industrial centers of the North, and the Atlantic and Pacific coasts. The other was the movement of many middle-class whites out of the city into the suburbs—the suburban revolution. These movements have left the city as it is today with a very different kind of population composition. The inner city is now very largely devoted to nonwhites, and to the impoverished groups who have missed out—on freedom, on jobs, on power, on income. They came to the cities originally for the same thing that has drawn people to cities for centuries—looking for work and excitement, and for other people of their own kind.

If I may quote myself, I did an unconscionably long article (Lerner, 1968) for the quarterly scholarly magazine, *Daedalus,* in an issue called *The Conscience of the City*—an article called "The Negro American and His City." The subtitle I used was "Person in Place in Culture." I think it is necessary to see not just the American Negro, but other Americans, too, in these terms—Person in Place in Culture. What the American Negro wants and needs is a sense of himself as a person, his identity and worth, his dignity and pride. But he is not an atomistic individual. He is somewhere— in place, in that city and that neighborhood. He needs roots and pride in it. But he is also in culture. In two cultures, actually—his own, with its own tradition, and in the larger American culture. He needs freedom to move around. We need, along with him, to break the ghetto trap so that he can move around. But if he wants to stay wherever he wants to stay, he must find roots and a sense of identity and a pride in himself and in his cultural context.

I take basically an organic approach to the whole civilization process; I do not take a mechanistic approach. As persons we are organic beings and we live as part of organisms. The family is an organism, college is an organism, the city is an organism, the neighborhood is an organism, the society is an organism. You cannot tear an organism away from its roots. But neither can you treat an organism as if it were a mechanical thing.

It is only in the last few years that this has become the weight of my thinking. I am convinced that much of what is happening today is in violation of the organic health of the individual, the community, and the nation—which includes the inner city and the college campus. Oscar Lewis did a very famous, by now classic, book called *La Vida* (1966)', a study of Puerto Ricans both in Puerto Rico and New York City. He pointed out something we have very much taken to heart. I, by the way, came with my family from Russia and was of a Jewish ghetto, one of the older ghettos of New York City. There are the newer ghettos now, the black ghettos, the Puerto Rican ghettos, the Mexican-American ghettos, and so on. As Oscar Lewis points out, in both ghettos there was an economy of poverty. In the newer ghettos there is also cultural poverty. In the older ghettos there was no cultural poverty, there was a culture of richness. The difference is crucial, because in the family and neighborhood in which I grew up, while there was plenty of poverty, we had to hold together as a family against the hostile environment and it gave us a cohesiveness that many families today lack.

There are at least two distinctions between the older ghettos and the new ones: we in the older ghettos did not have the heritage of slavery to carry and we in the older ghettos did not have the badge of color. Those two distinctions make all the difference in the world. And that makes the whole process so much more difficult. If you look at what I call the career line of the young American Negro growing up in the ghetto, as you look through his early life, see what happens to him, what are the formative influences? The first: home or what counts as a home, in an unstructured family, with the most important single thing in it being the television set. Television has had a more revolutionary impact on the inner-city ghetto than on any other part of American life. For the first time they have a window to look out at society. The second has been the streets. The street has not always been—what shall we say, in our terms—antiseptic. There have been prostitution, dope addiction, rackets, violence. And the third is the school. The school has become very often an angry school, and an angry classroom, and all too often the young Negro child commutes between the world of the school, a middle-class world, and the world of the home and the street, which is not a middle-class world.

But outside of all of them, through the TV set, he sees the larger society. And what does he see? He sees the Babylonian surfaces of our life. He sees the opulence of it. And if he were not sufficiently convinced of the opulence by what he sees in the ordinary shows on TV, the commercials convince him. He sees instantism: everything is presented to him as something you get instantly. The commercial products especially are instant, but so are the stories, about people who want things instantly, and instantism is one of the lessons that he learns. He stretches out his hands to this opulent, sensual, affluent society wanting to get some of it instantly and it recedes. Like Tantalus, of the Greek myth, he stretches out his hands and the opulence recedes—and the result is rage.

Tocqueville has pointed out, in his study of the French revolution, that great revolutions come in societies not when the condition of the people is at its worst, but when the condition is improving. And that pretty much has been true in terms of the inner city—conditions have actually been improving. In the beginning, before these new revolutionary changes, there was hopelessness, along with a certain apathy and sullenness. That hopelessness was replaced by hope. But the trouble is that the hope has not been fulfilled. It has been anything but fulfilled. The result has been frustration along with the hope. The question for the future is whether we can have hope without frustration, because hope with frustration results in rage. If we do not want rage, we must offer both hope and some chance of fulfilling that hope—without frustration—and the rages will die out. I do not expect that to happen soon.

What is needed is perspective—a very long-time view of the whole process by which the blacks in America can come into the real inheritance of American life. That is going to take some time. The only chance we have of avoiding violence on a larger scale is by making sure that this process becomes a more credible one. I think we are working at it; that is about the best I can say. People have often asked, what is the essence of this whole process of minority groups becoming part of the larger American structure? I had an interesting experience. I was in India for a year teaching. I came back by way of eastern Europe and I stopped off at Warsaw for awhile. Some of the writers and other intellectuals there had a kind of evening for me. The chairman of the evening got up; he said, "Mr. Lerner, you've written this massive book on American civilization. We haven't had a chance to have it translated, but could you tell us in a single word what is the essence of American civilization?"

"It's a book of a thousand pages," I said, "you want a thousand pages distilled into one word?"

"Yes," he said, "would you?"

Have you ever had this thrown at you, in one word what is America? I thought very hard, very fast, what is it? Is it freedom, is it democracy, is it equality, is it tolerance, is it decency, is it justice, is it dynamism, is it enterprise? Suddenly almost to my surprise I heard myself say: "Access."

The chairman laughed. He said, "We've heard a lot about American *suc*cess, we hadn't heard of *ac*cess."

"You see," I said, "we have a Declaration of Independence that says all men are born free and equal. I hope we're born free and we'll remain free; we're not born equal, we're born with very unequal abilities and potentials. Every employer knows it, every teacher knows it, every parent knows it. I have a brood of children of my own and every one of them was born unequal. But," I said, "we also have the notion that there ought to be equal access to equal life chances, so that every unequally born youngster gets the chance to develop his unequal ability to the fullest. It is in this sense that access is the heart of the American experience."

I do not know of any definition of *access* that elaborates it clearly. It means equal chance at equal life chances. We have to break into the ghettos to give people in the inner city that kind of equal chance. We have to make sure that they are no longer at the bottom of the pyramid. We have to make sure that the things they have been without, they will no longer be without—without power, without money incomes, without jobs, without skills, without a cultural tradition that they can be proud of, without a sense of identity. If I had to choose from these I would say the crucial ones have to do with money, to give them income, by getting jobs and skills. That would be number one. Number two is power. Some kind of participation in what is happening around them. Third is education in order to be able to prepare themselves. And fourth is a sense of identity.

I do not know whether I would order those things in just that sequence, but I do know my reactions to some of the efforts now being made in these directions by the more urgent groups among black Americans. For example, they put an enormous stress on power. And I can understand it, since they have been powerless. I can even understand black power, by the way, and commend it very much. For example, in Los Angeles during the spring 1969 campaign I was on the same platform with Tom Bradley, who was running for mayor. I was very happy to have a chance to support him in his race there with Sam Yorty. I think it would have been wonderful to have had that kind of man—that kind of man, not meaning white or black, but with his kind of experience and integrity and character—as mayor of Los Angeles. The fact that he is black makes it all the better, because in a symbolic way it points to the possibility of black power in the best sense—as in Cleveland with Stokes, in Gary with Hatcher, in Washington, D.C., in Massachusetts with Brooks, or on the Supreme Court with Thurgood Marshall.

This is black power, for me. But not black power in a prescriptive way. I do not like black power that is prescriptive just as I do not like white power that is prescriptive. I do not like black supremacy, just as I do not like white supremacy. But I do very much believe the powerlessness of the American blacks has to be replaced by a sharing of power.

I have the same feeling, basically, about identity. I think one of the healthiest things that has developed in recent years has been the whole thrust toward pride of identity. I know that I never really came to terms with myself as a person until I had come to terms with the whole question of my ethnic origins as a Jew, the whole feeling of facing that, of trying to resolve what seemed for awhile conflicting claims between the subculture and the larger American culture. Eventually, I think I faced it and resolved it. Whoever has tried to do that knows the increased strength, the increased fertility, creativeness he gets from the process. This must be true of American blacks as well. They need a sense of pride in their ethnic identity, but this again must not be prescriptive. It is not a question of having to hate the whites in order to feel that black is beautiful. It is not necessary to say to the whites, "You've got to give us back what you've taken." I do not think that basically the problem is one of direct restitution. I do not think the induced sense of guilt that results from such demands is a very healthy thing. The problem is the rebuilding of a society—going on with the series of changes, within the frame of consent, which will make it possible for blacks and whites to find out who they are, to achieve their potential, and to live together.

And the same applies to the so-called generational struggle, or generational confrontation. The university is an arena today, more and more, as every college president knows. I have come to believe that the most dangerous single occupation in the United States today is that of being a college president, without much question. There is only one other that compares with it at all— being a parent. I think both of them are dangerous, and dangerous in very similar ways, because both deal with growing organisms. Both have the obligation to make sure these organisms are not hurt beyond retrieval. Both have the obligation to try to create some kind of frame, within which changes and growth can take place, and within which the growth of freedom can take place. In that sense the two occupations have very real parallels.

I have been a teacher for a long time; I have had a succession of what I might call generations of students. I began teaching in 1932. In the 1930s, I remember, my students were very socially conscious. In the 1940s they were very career conscious. In the 1950s they were unconscious. If I had to make a choice between their being unconscious and what has happened to them in the 1960s, I think I would choose the 1960s, when they are very intensely socially conscious again, as in the 1930s. But I think I would say to them, as I have said to students for some time now, the question is not just are you socially conscious; the question is what do you do with it, where do you go, how do you do it?

You see there are two universes that we live in when we talk of the generational conflict. One is the outer universe, the objective universe, and that applies to all of us; young and old, black and white, the objective universe is the same for all of us. But the other is the inner universe, the subjective universe, the universe of our own inner minds and spirits, the window through which we look out at the outer universe. When I talk to my students, when I talk to my own sons, I know that our outer universe is the same but our inner universes are very different because mine was shaped in the breakdown of our economy, it was shaped during the Spanish Civil War, it was shaped during the shadow of Nazism over the world and we saw the consequences of what happened when the Weimer Republic was allowed to be destroyed. It was shaped at that time. It was shaped in the whole postwar era with our efforts to do something about Communist expansionism. That was when my inner universe was shaped. My sons and students do not remember it. They were not alive then. They do not remember and on the whole they do not really care. They are not history-minded, they are not past-minded. One of the efforts I have to make as a teacher is to try to say that it is very difficult to do very much about the present and the future unless you try to learn something about what happened in the past, but this is not true of them. And the result is, of course, that it is difficult to communicate—and why should it not be difficult to communicate?

I think two things are crucial—one is communication itself, and the other is trust. One of the things I say about the Lerner household, if I may be a little personal, is that the most important single article of furniture in the Lerner household is the kitchen refrigerator. The reason for that is, as my sons have grown up and been out late, and may I say they have been out late, when they come back, I do not ask where they have been, what they have done, or say that when I was young we did it so-and-so. I am there, also sitting up pretty late. We go to the kitchen, we raid the refrigerator, we sit down at the kitchen table, we talk. And I try to listen; I try to help them learn the art of listening, which is not very easy. One of the things I try to say to them is, "Look, there are many

38

things we disagree on, but I want you to know something. No matter what our differences may be, there's never anything you can do to make me break my trust in you. And I hope there's nothing I'll be able to do to make you break your trust in me. Because if we lose trust there can be no communication. Communication is only an empty jangling of sounds. If we can retain trust, I think we can restore communication."

But, of course, what is happening now is that the trust itself is being broken. It is being broken between the racial groups, it is being broken now between the generations.

I think it is rather crucial for us to understand both the short-run and the long-run things that can be done, that must be done, about that kind of violence on the college campuses. And while this comes very largely from some of the militant black groups, it comes also from the white radicals, so-called New Left, the SDS, which, in turn, is dominated by one of its own minorities, Progressive Labor, which is Maoist oriented, Casker White oriented. Mr. Garelik, who used to be chief inspector of the New York police and ran with John Lindsay in the mayoralty race, gave an interview during that race in which he said something about the funds from abroad that some of these radical student movements get. Because the reaction was very sharp and swift, Mayor Lindsay made him withdraw what he had said. I do not think, I do not know that there are funds from abroad. I do not think it is important. I do not think funds are the important thing, but I think the objectives are important. And for a group like Progressive Labor there is very little question that the objectives are not to make the college better, not to rebuild the college, but to destroy the college. The objective is to try to use the Negro situation in the colleges, use them as allies if possible, and try to reach through them the Negro mass in the inner city; this is part of their basic theory of revolution. They are serious about revolution in America in the first sense—the classical, historical sense. It is part of their basic theory of revolution that the revolutionary group today is two: one, the Negro masses, and second, the intellectuals in the colleges.

One of the things they share with some of the more militant

of the Negro groups that have been violent on the campuses has been the feeling that if the objective is high enough, then the means do not matter. And in terms of means, anything goes. The true believer is so certain that he has a pipeline to the divine, the infinite, that he need not worry about the means he uses. And in the case both of the black militants, especially those who have used guns as at Cornell, and of the Progressive Labor group, and the SDS, this is true. I have tried to say several things to these young people on a succession of college campuses as I have talked with them. The first thing I have said is, "Look, I'm glad to see your activism, I believe in activism. Why don't you go back to what Henri Bergson once said what he was asked to give a paper at a congress of philosophers, and couldn't give a paper. He sent a message of a single sentence. The message read, 'Act as men of thought, think as men of action.' " What I say to these young people is, "Sure, act, but act out a context of reflective thinking. Act as men of thought. Otherwise your action will be blind and destructive. And, yes, you're here at college to think. It's very good to think as men of action, very, very good, but make sure you make the connection between thought and action." The second thing I say to them is, "Look, if you are really revolutionary, then you'd better take the consequences."

When the SDS group walked out of Fayrweather Hall at Columbia, when they were served with an injunction and they decided to vacate Fayrweather Hall, they covered their faces with their coats, as if they were Mafia operators, for example, who did not want the disgrace of notoriety. But surely these young people, if they are revolutionaries, ought to take *pride* in being revolutionaries. I do not think they can have it both ways. And if they are going to be revolutionaries, they had better not expect society to accommodate them, either the administrators or faculty of the universities, or the officials of the society. There is no suicide impulse built into America. If they are really going to be revolutionaries, then the final issue is a showdown of power. There are some, by the way, who feel this way. I do not know how many. The story is that among the Bolsheviks that took over power in Russia, there

Max Lerner

were no more than a few tens of thousands. But, of course, what was true of Russia was that the rest of society was in collapse, that those who were governing were no longer able to govern, and those who were being governed were unwilling to be governed. I do not think that these conditions are true of American society. And I think that most of the revolutionary theory we are hearing today does not reckon with these facts.

I say one more thing to these young people—I say, "I've got three questions for you. What is your heroism, what is your *1)* notion of what is heroic, and who do you think is the enemy? That's number one. We knew who the enemy was in the days when I was at college and a young instructor, and I think we located the enemy in a crucial way. The enemy was concentrated power, the enemy was poverty, the enemy was Nazism, and so on. I think we knew who, what our heroism was. Secondly, what are your limits? What *2)* means do you use and where do you stop? Or is there no place where you stop? And third, what is your Jerusalem? Remember *3)* William Blake said, 'We must build Jerusalem on England's green and shining land.' What is your Jerusalem?"

Sometimes I get answers to the first, I do not get answers to the second, I very rarely get answers to the third about Jerusalem.

There are some very real questions that we have to ask and I want to end with this one: What are they doing? Why do they do it? And instead of trying to find a particular answer, I have rounded up some theories as to why they do it. About seven of them. There are three that have to do with the society itself.

One theory is that this society is too affluent. Because it is affluent, there has not been any real confrontation forced on these young people in their early years, with poverty, with difficulties. They have no memory of social reality. There is no willingness, in psychiatric terms, to face the reality principle, which means postponing present gratification for future needs. The second is that America is a sick society, a violent society. The violence is built in. It is built into the very nature of our society. It is to be found in the wars that we wage and do not seem to be able to stop. It is built into our nuclear weapons, and it spills over into the thinking

41

of the young. The third theory is that our society has an empty value structure. The values we teach and preach are not very rewarding. They are not very nutritive to the young, who do not believe in them.

There are two theories that have to do with the American family. One is that the family has been too permissive—David Riesman says this generation of college students is the first generation that was picked up when they cried as babies—permissive in that sense, with a desire for instant gratification. The second family theory is that the problem is not a permissive family structure but a too-repressive, partly family and partly social structure, that there has not been enough freedom for genuine personal theories of what happens in the growing up years, that there has been a distortion of identification, that the young people who need someone to identify with have not had a healthy identification model. The father, for example, was the healthy model for a boy in the earlier republic. The boy knew what the father was doing. He was proud of it. He identified with the father's work. He often followed him. That is no longer true. The boy rarely knows what it is that the father does, does not have a chance really to identify with the work or with the father, and cuts himself away from his father. The father is not often around and even when he is around, his emotional and intellectual authority is not there. This means a distortion of identification in the sense that since there is no real object to identify with, when the rebellion phase comes, it is directed not against the identification object, but against the whole society, against the older generation.

And finally, there is the Bettelheim theory of protracted adolescence: what has been happening is a longer educational track; that while puberty is a biological fact, adolescence is not a biological but a social fact. That the years after puberty are very long years which the young people spend waiting, waiting for something that never happens. They are not moving into the immediate process of some of their predecessors in previous generations, of jobs and raising families, but waiting, waiting—a little like waiting for Godot.

I do not know which of these theories is valid. I suspect

there is some truth is most of them. I think we would have to draw some kind of circle through them to see what part of each of them could be included with some kind of consistency in a single circle. My own emphasis would be on the identification, the absence of the reality principle in their lives, and the long process of adolescence. We cannot deal with these young people on the college campuses as if they were so much material to manipulate. They are organisms. They are the real growth material of our society. The question is how to create some kind of a setting within which they can carry on this learning process and teaching process in a healthy way. This means, as I suggested, growing some kind of circle outside of which they cannot go. And that means the student bodies and the faculty and the administration in every college must learn how to hold together, to reach decisions together. It means the colleges must be kept open and not closed down. It means the police must not be called except as a last resort. That does not mean, by the way, never called, because the time may come when there is no other way. It means the injunction process, which has been used so very well at the University of Chicago and at Columbia. It means that even more basically the colleges themselves—as organisms—must use their own laws of life. The ultimate sanction must be the college sanction in terms of suspension or exclusion. Young people are always not only welcome, they are nurtured; we cherish them on the campus, but not if they want to destroy the organism of the university. Those who want to destroy the organism of the university have to take the consequences.

But while this is happening one other process must happen: and that is we must move into a new era of constitution-making on the university campuses, because the political structure of the university has grown archaic. Just as surely as we needed a new era in the late 1780s for our political fabric as a nation, so we need a new era of constitution-making on the campuses, with the tripartite pooling of decision-making by all groups involved.

I still call myself a possibilist. I think these things can be done if we use collective intelligence and collective will. As I have moved around the country recently more and more people have said to me, "Mr. Lerner, up there in space, do you think there's intelligent life? And do you think we'll ever be able to communicate with intelligent life in space?" And I say, "That's a fascinating question, but I have another question of a higher order of priority. Not is there intelligent life up there in space, but is there intelligent life down here on earth? And not will we ever be able to communicate with space, but will we ever be able to communicate with each other—nation with nation, race with race, generation with generation?"

Willis E. Dugan

Opportunity
for All

3

Is it possible for colleges to provide for the disadvantaged along with the gifted? Let me say at the beginning that it is not only possible, but absolutely necessary, if we are to maintain a productive society and effective educational experience for the full range of children, youth, and adults. I do not mean to imply that extending the concept of equal educational opportunity will be smooth or problem-free; on the contrary, many difficulties exist, many difficulties are present at this time.

45

Educational opportunity for all is not a new goal in American education. Indeed, the principle—if not the practice—of equal rights for all our citizens is deeply rooted in our nation's history. However, in practice, we have not always provided sufficient opportunities for persons to realize equality; and we acknowledge that the concept of equal educational opportunity has carried various meanings depending on the historical era, minority populations under discussion, stage of our economic development, and society's shifting interests, not to mention the political scene. The concept has altered considerably in recent years to focus attention on the disadvantaged—primarily urban and primarily black—although many other demographic groupings should be logically included.

We have long acknowledged that education is the principal means by which an individual has an opportunity to change his life style and to provide for a better life, and, in the aggregate, it is the principal means by which a society makes progress. As we develop an individual through education, we prepare him for life and for a vocation. Although it has not always been evident in our society at large, we in education, at least, have long adhered to the principle of the value of all productive work, irrespective of the status of occupation. This is, in turn, a reflection of our belief in the worth and the dignity of the individual and in his opportunity.

Historically, equal educational opportunity in the United States is not a new concept. The origins go back to the early nineteenth century. This movement was well nurtured in the United States by our relatively open class structure and it focused on equality from its very beginnings.

In the twentieth century, the term *higher education* has come to be applied to a great variety of post-secondary institutions of learning, including not only universities and colleges but also large numbers of professional schools, teacher-training schools, junior colleges (a peculiarly American institution), institutes of technology, and so on. In taking over the established forms of higher education from Western Europe, the American people have broadened and democratized them so that more and more persons have the opportunity to obtain some form of post-secondary training.

In 1900, only about 10 per cent of high school age youth were in school; about 75 per cent of those who graduated went on to college. However, by the 1950s, 90 per cent of all children of high school age were in school—reflecting almost universal secondary education. Of this, a more heterogeneous group of about 25 to 35 per cent went on to college. In 1968, there were approximately seven million college students; in comparison to earlier figures of all youth ages thirteen to twenty-one, while 5 per cent were attending college in 1910, nearly 50 to 55 per cent were attending post-secondary education in 1968.

The great growth of educational opportunity was enhanced by those activities, programs, and developments that occurred in the middle of the twentieth century after World War II.

The Servicemen's Readjustment Act of 1944, better known as the "GI Bill of Rights," enabled masses of returning veterans to attend college who would not otherwise have had the opportunity for academic study beyond the secondary school. Enrollments grew enormously. In 1939, 1,365,000 students were enrolled in institutions of higher education. In 1946, when higher education first felt the impact of the veterans, enrollments climbed to 2,078,000. By the late 1950s, enrollments exceeded three million and by the mid-1960s, approximately six million. Veteran's privileges were extended in 1952 to Korean War veterans and in 1966 to veterans of the Vietnam conflict.

In this post-Sputnik period (since 1958)', we have seen enormous growth in our national priority for education. President Johnson, signing the Higher Education Act amendments and the Vocational-Technical Education Act amendments in 1968, indicated that there had been ninety pieces of educational legislation put on the statutes in the period of the three Democratic administrations.

The National Defense Education Act (1959) included loans to students in its provisions. (Its impact, however, was reduced by its loyalty oath provision.) The Elementary and Secondary Education

Act of 1965 and the Higher Education Act of 1965 marked a historical change in the federal government's role. The latter provided: aid to small colleges and developing institutions through cooperative programs and national teaching fellowships, with exchange faculty members, exchange students, visiting scholars, and sharing of libraries and laboratories; grants for libraries and library training and research; support of community service and continuing education programs; and federal scholarships (under equal opportunity grants), student loan programs, and work-study opportunities. Obviously, any listing of this kind of development within the area of higher education makes it perfectly clear that there has been a strong effort on the part of state and local governments and the federal government to support the extension of education to a broader range and spectrum of society.

The disadvantaged have always been with us but today we are more aware of them because we are experiencing a broad national concern about pressing societal problems. Increasingly, *disadvantaged* has come to mean the poor urban black, although all of us can identify many other eligible populations: migrant workers, stationary rural poor, and American Indians are three. The term *disadvantaged* implies a large cluster of deficiencies and inadequate experiences. Low socioeconomic status causes problems for an individual in nearly every aspect of life—from personal health and marginal living conditions to poor self-concepts and insufficient opportunities to participate. The implication for education is that youth must be assisted in as many ways as needed to be as successful and productive as possible in our society.

In a broad sense, the need today is for early identification of talent, relevant and enabling compensatory educational programs, more flexible admissions approaches, institutional alternatives and experimental programs, innovative curricula, opportunities for student participation in decision-making, large-scale financial support for students and institutions, careful advisory and counseling services, new student recruitment efforts, and new directions in the extracurriculum.

As an aside at this point, may I say that one of the principal

48

concepts for which I hold considerable feeling is the need for a broader perception of talent, the fact that so often within this country and within the educational structure, elementary, secondary, or post-secondary, we have a narrow perception of talent. Talent is often thought of in terms of quantitative terms alone, rather than in human terms. A talent is often thought of as a high degree of mathematical ability, or a high test score; rather talent must be looked for in terms of intraindividual differences as well as inter-individual differences, and I would submit that those of us who are looking for equal educational opportunities for all should consider the peaks of talent that may exist irrespective of test scores, irrespective of special attributes that might have been viewed narrowly as talent.

The basic priority today should be to provide superior and creative educational offerings and services in order to allow disadvantaged youth to compete fairly. Academic standards need not be sacrificed and advantaged students will not suffer from the attention paid to the needs of the disadvantaged; in fact, the educational experiences of all our students will be enhanced by careful attention to new programs and new directions of meeting the needs of the disadvantaged. The university could be an experimental microcosm of the kind of aware, knowledgeable, and pluralistic society-at-large we hope to see in this nation's future—a nation where the rewards of an open society are available to and shared by all. It should be anticipated by now that this large-scale effort will require a major share of our national and economic resources. It will be an investment well made.

Colleges and universities cannot be expected to make up for long-term educational deficiencies, however, and ideally the innovations and interventions necessary to equalize educational opportunities should be initiated as early as possible. Pre-college curricula and programs need to be redesigned and diversified in order to provide for varying futures. Alternatives to higher education need to be emphasized. Universities need to generate new and transform old institutional forms—of program and of organization. New links need to be established to community needs, to work, to interdisciplinary combined arts and professional preparation programs, that meet the needs of a complex society.

What are we doing now to equalize and extend educational opportunities? Many programs and new forms of education have either emerged over the last five years or significantly expanded.

Programs of compensatory education are now operating at all educational levels. Head Start for preschool youngsters and Upward Bound for students hoping to attend college are two of the better known federally sponsored ones. Additional federal programs designed primarily as services to youngsters classified as disadvantaged include the Job Corps, Neighborhood Youth Corps, Youth Opportunity Centers, and the like.

Of the programs just mentioned, the outcomes of Upward Bound are particularly relevant to our emphasis upon higher education. In operation since 1965, Upward Bound projects enrolling some 26,000 students have operated at 300 colleges and universities in the past four years. The program seems successful in its stated attempts to motivate, to raise the aspirations, and to teach disadvantaged high school youngsters as attested to by the fact that 80 per cent of the 12,000 who have finished Upward Bound training have been admitted to college; of this group, 67 per cent have remained in college. Most of these students had high school grade averages of *C* or *D* prior to the program and were bored with school and its irrelevant education. Some were high school dropouts and many had police records. The program demonstrates that low-achieving youngsters living in poverty are more capable of learning than their records indicate or their teachers believe. It is not possible to attribute the program's success to any single factor; rather it is a combination of things. Perhaps the most important program feature for us to note in relation to possible accommodations that colleges can make is that the program required change on the parts of all who participated—the youngsters, college administrators and faculty, high school teachers, and undergraduate colleagues. The program required new ways of doing new things for persons previously locked into a given structure.

Willis E. Dugan

There are many new or expanding forms of educational organization which are helping to meet the need for increased educational opportunity. Of them, the growth of the junior college is the most striking phenomenon. With about fifty new ones opening each year, they are the fastest growing form of institution in American education. A twentieth-century creation, they usually offer both liberal arts and vocational courses and are increasingly coming to be known as community colleges. These colleges will increasingly assume responsibility for preparing students to enter the junior year of senior institutions. In addition, these colleges are providing the kind of vocational education or occupational education which should help satisfy our national shortages of technicians and skilled industrial employees. The junior colleges also offer adults the opportunity for continuing education and occupational retraining. They will be a bright hope for the relatively disadvantaged of the future because, through this type of institution, many of tomorrow's students will have a chance for the kind of education which is being denied to most of their counterparts of today. The phenomenal growth of community colleges in urban areas no doubt will be accompanied by many complex problems, but this movement is establishing the direction for extending public education at least two years beyond high school.

Another kind of institution which holds promise for the future is the urban university. Existing ones are increasingly becoming involved in programs for the disadvantaged and culturally deprived. In addition, we would expect new ones to develop as more public attention is focused on, and public support developed for, the needs of urban areas. This emphasis would be today's counterpart to the rural bias which has influenced higher educational development over the past century.

The experimental college has a particularly important role in American higher education today. A related recent development is the cluster college, or smaller college unit (often residential), within the larger institution. It attempts to combine the assets of the large university and the unique climate of the small college.

Finally, opportunities for post-secondary education and training other than through institutions of higher education should not be overlooked. I refer particularly to the expanding of vocational and technical education. The need for tremendous numbers and a higher proportion of youth to go into post-secondary education which is essentially skilled training and preparation for business, industry, and meeting the economic needs of this nation. Business, industry, the military, the federal government and specialized schools are continuing to offer greater opportunities for comprehensive continuing education and training programs to meet the needs of the job market.

What do all these efforts mean and what do they add up to? How can we best provide equal educational opportunities on a massive level for our disadvantaged youth with college potential?

The programs and forms of education just reviewed constitute the initial phase of our fight for new opportunities for today's disadvantaged. There are problems, to be sure. These attempts are fragmented and uncoordinated. Thousands of programs must exist around the country which never are communicated to the academic community at large. Their lack of conformity is a strength, of course. American higher education has never conformed to one uniform pattern, whether of organization, administration, or support. However, program and organizational results must be soundly evaluated and more widely shared.

Finally, a tangential concern is the relationship of campus disturbances to the struggle for equal educational opportunity. Certainly the rising aspirations of all students for experimental programs, for a share and a voice in the decision-making for a relevant education, the demand of minority students for immediate access to higher education, and the desire of various radical groups for greater recognition of their contributions to American life, are contributory factors and cannot be overlooked.

The genuine progress and the long-range goals of higher education require much cooperation. I refer briefly to two national reports. The Carnegie Commission on Education (1968) identifies

Willis E. Dugan

fourteen federal aid proposals geared to improving both academic quality and equality of opportunity in higher education. Those recommendations of particular relevance to achieving goals of equality fall under the category of student aid and related institutional grants. They include strengthening and expanding the present program of educational opportunity grants, establishing a program of supplementary matching grants, providing federal scholarship grants to institutions, incorporating the college work-study program into this overall proposal, expanding the present federal aid program of guidance, counseling, and testing, establishing a doctoral fellowship program, and creating a national student loan bank. The total cost of the various federal aid programs recommended in the Report would be almost $7 billion in 1970–71 and would rise to almost $13 billion in 1976–77. The current cost of comparable federal aid programs is now $3.5 billion.

In addition, the Department of Health, Education, and Welfare (1969) has stated that federal aid to higher education in the future should promote equality of opportunity by insuring that all able students can afford to go on to post-secondary education and that institutions are able to accommodate them.

Inequality will always be present, given the nature of man and society. However, it is encouraging that the American people have become aware of the glaring deficiencies in the availability of the necessities of life—and some form of higher education or technical training is quickly becoming a necessity in this complex society.

In sum, educational changes in our institutions of higher education and in society will be required if the goal of educational opportunity for all is going to be realized. Innovative programs will have to emerge from these changes. I have attempted to highlight some of these new directions and possibilities in this paper. I see the decade ahead as one of necessary readjustment and turmoil. Our greatest challenge is to develop each individual to the full extent of his potential and thus to allow for greater improvements in the quality of our lives and our society.

53

Commentary

Leo A. Munday

It is clear that our society needs more black college graduates, that they must enter the mainstream of life, and that these are two different things. Developing effective college programs for blacks takes more than money and good intentions. One problem is a research deficit. The educational research in the area has not shown an outline of the relationships among the major factors in the field. Education is only one of several social agencies involved in inequality of opportunity and this makes it hard for movement to take place in one area. It is easy to refer to "they" or "them" or "something that they are doing" because it is hard to make progress at many points. It has recently been documented in the book *Beyond High School* (Trent and Medsker, 1968) that students who go to college are more tolerant than students who do not go to college. So perhaps such a role for the college is realistic.

Allan W. Ostar

On the matter of national public policy, the question here is how best to provide educational opportunity for all—by giving the money to the students or by giving the money to institutions to enable them to expand educational opportunity? The Carnegie Commission reports and also the HEW Committee on Federal Support would expand the equality of opportunity by allocating a substantial part of federal higher education funds directly to students. Both these committees have acknowledged that this will enable institutions to raise their tuitions more readily. The inevitable consequence, of course, is an escalation process which would require ever-increasing student financial aid funds to enable students to meet the ever-increasing costs of going to college. This trend, I believe, would lead down the road to the point where the student would bear the primary burden for the support of higher education. In response to the position that students should pay a much greater share of educational cost, Howard Bowen estimates that in real economic terms the student already is paying about 75 per cent of the cost of going to college when you take into account foregone earnings. Bowen's analysis brings him to the conclusion that the recent rise in tuition, in both public and private institutions, should not continue and that the further escalation of tuition is essentially unsound. He proposes a national program based on aid to students to help them meet college costs and aid to their institutions to keep the college charges from rising. There is research evidence available that students have a better chance at institutions with flexible admissions policies and relatively low tuition charges than at institutions with large financial aid programs. California and New Jersey are extreme examples. In California, about 80 per cent or more of all high school graduates go on to some kind of post-secondary higher education. In New Jersey, only about 30 per cent of the high school graduates go on to post-secondary education. In California, students as they come into high school know there is an institution somewhere in that state where they can go and which they can afford. In New Jersey, the expectation level of high school graduates is relatively low because of the limited amount of educational opportunity available both in terms of cost and the number of spaces available. We are engaged in a debate now that is not unlike that at the turn of the century involving free public high schools. Should the truck driver pay taxes so that the youngster in Greenfield Hills can have his education subsidized? We settled that point in favor of the free public high school. We have talked about universal education opportunity beyond the high school but we are back to the old argument about who should pay, society or the individual, in terms of who is the principal beneficiary, the society or the individual? It is a good investment for society to have everyone go to college to acquire an education to the limit of his ability because he will more than pay back the cost of that education out of the increased taxes that would be generated.

Nevitt Sanford

Loss of
Talent

4

I would like to start by distinguishing between loss of talent as a manpower problem and loss of talent as a human problem.

The manpower problem, as ordinarily stated, lies in discovering and developing what are sometimes called the human resources necessary for the achievement of more or less agreed national goals. This problem was very well defined for us after Sputnik, when a flurry of publications on talent loss, talent discovery and identification, and excellence appeared. But this has been, I believe, a traditional interest of the elite colleges, which are concerned with the production of professionals. Traditionally, too, the testing industry has been concerned with serving this interest.

As a human problem, the question is how do we develop the talents of the individual so that he might fulfill himself and gratify his distinctively human needs. I should say that personality development depends heavily upon the development of the individual's talents, just as a talent, in its manifestations, depends upon the total development of the person. In a way, I am drawing a distinction between the notion that the individual exists for society and the notion that society exists for the individual. When the chips go down, I favor the latter alternative.

Ideally, the two kinds of talent development would go together. If we developed everybody's talents as fully as possible, or as fully as could be justified on the basis of their needs, then the work of society would get done perfectly all right. But if the two should come into conflict, I would give priority to the humanistic goal. The fact is—and this seems to me of enormous importance—that what talents actually get developed in our society, or in any society, depend upon the developmental status of the society and also upon public policy.

It is clear that in our industrialized society certain kinds of talents are becoming more or less irrelevant. It is hard to find bookbinders, tailors, printers, and other craftsmen of various kinds. There is simply little place for them in a society such as ours. There may be, on the other hand, places for them in the new hippie communities of the sort that are being started in northern New Mexico. There, presumably, they will develop talents for music and interpersonal relations, whereas in our society today, the accent is on producing technicians to run an enormous technological complex—computer experts, data analysts, and the like.

I am not suggesting that our galloping technology is a bad thing. Obviously, it should be subjected to better control, but it has led to a state of affairs in which there is less need for labor, more leisure for most people, more and more opportunities for people to develop their human potentialities and to perform all

57

kinds of services for other people. We have a chance for great movement in the direction of universal higher education or full development for everybody, primarily because our technology has been so productive.

What happens depends also, of course, on public policy—fundamentally, on what are believed to be major national goals. It is interesting to recall, now, that right after World War II there was a big movement on the mental health front—attention having been drawn to the psychological problems of draftees and of returning veterans. Vast national programs were started, involving all the helping professions, particularly psychiatry and clinical psychology. All kinds of people-oriented activities were accented for a period in the late forties and early fifties. Now all this is changed, the accent having switched to national defense. Accordingly, clinical psychology has receded into the background while experimental psychology has come to the fore as a part of a fresh accent on science in general.

Consider in this same connection the state of affairs in socialist countries, particularly those that are relatively undeveloped, where all available manpower is always needed. Every effort goes into developing the talents needed to keep the machinery going. In such countries, discrimination on the basis of race, or sex, or age even, cannot be afforded. Hence, in the Soviet Union we find women not only sweeping the streets but also acting as directors of great research laboratories. In India, more women than men are serving as physicians, whereas in our country women, and members of other minorities, are the last to be drawn into production. In wartime, however, we put all hands to work, and then it becomes clear that we have an enormous amount of talent that is not ordinarily used. In World War II it was demonstrated that poor southern Negroes could learn how to build ships almost overnight. And we have always known that women can do anything that needs doing. But the fact of the matter is that now these groups are the last to enter into the general realm of higher education.

It is still true that three out of five high school graduates who never go to college are women; if we consider the number of qualified blacks who fail to enter college, we find that the figures previously reported by Coleman (1966) still hold true: while blacks constitute 11 per cent of our total population, they still make up less than 3 per cent of the college population. The fact is, of course, that when poorly prepared black students do get into college, they do quite well. I think it is fair to say, after Pearson (1966), that a full cross-section of high school graduates is now represented in our colleges. People in the lower quarter of the ability spectrum stay in college, as well as, if not better than, anybody else. The most obvious waste of talent concerns women, particularly their failure to undertake higher degrees. Moynihan (1966), basing his estimates on Bureau of Labor statistics, pointed out that in 1960, only one-tenth of the women who were qualified to obtain higher degrees—qualified by virtue of basic ability—actually went on to obtain those degrees.

The reason for this, in my opinion, is that talent is felt not to be needed to achieve agreed national goals. Nonetheless, the development of talent for its own sake is valued in the United States. There is a widespread feeling, however, that this ought not be done at public expense, but that it ought to be a free enterprise. If the hippies want to do it in New Mexico, that is okay. But public monies, it is believed, ought to be devoted to developing those talents which are in the public interest. This usually means in the interest of goals which are agreed to by politicians, or which politicians believe will be approved by large constituencies. That is why we so often have to disguise our purposes. In recent years, for example, the U.S. Department of Labor has developed enormous programs to provide for the people at the bottom of the socioeconomic heap. But these had to be disguised as job training in the interest of national defense, or related objectives, because the American public is not ready to accept the idea that you develop people just because they are people.

If there were a rational national policy, that is to say, if we trained people in accord with actual national needs rather than in accord with those that can be put across to the American people through our politicians, a whole new range of talents would naturally be developed. For example, if we focused on urban development or on reducing the rate of infant mortality, the need for women would become much greater than it is now. But, in the light of our overproduction and poor distribution of goods, we can not argue for this sort of talent development on the basis of our stated national needs. Thus, we can anticipate a continuing great loss of talent until it becomes agreed that that development of people is an end in itself.

My next point is that neither our manpower needs nor our human needs are being adequately met through current practices in education. If asked to define talent I would say that it is a kind of potentiality. It is certainly not a fixed entity, possessed by some and not others. Talent is a state of the whole person, not something in the person that is specific to a particular kind of performance; in other words, we rarely can ascribe performance in some particular task to some particular talent that the individual is supposed to have. In my view, almost any worthwhile performance depends upon a very general and diffuse state in the whole person.

In this respect music, art, and mathematics may be somewhat special. But outside of those areas, when creative people have been compared with noncreative people, they have been found to differ in a full range of personality characteristics, not only with respect to some particular kind of ability factor. I also take the view that most children have the potential for most worthwhile endeavors. In other words, without denying the importance of genetic factors, I tend to side with Watson and Skinner in placing the emphasis on environmental factors: theoretically almost anything worth doing can be done, given the human material that is present at birth. The quality of the art of preliterate peoples and their extraordinary achievements support this position. Along these lines, I believe that most college graduates can still enter almost any field: the determination is not all that fixed. Almost any college graduate could still become a perfectly good doctor, if this were decided upon by all concerned. Furthermore, I maintain that failures in performance among graduate students are not due mainly to their inability at the time of entrance. There is plenty of ability among graduate students. If they do not perform the reason has most to do with what happens after they get to graduate school.

So I am an environmentalist, and an optimist by nature and by conviction. I do admit, however, that irreversible changes can occur as a result of malnutrition or of severe emotional deprivation in childhood. But in the main, the possibilities are still there after childhood and even after college entrance.

Talent loss in the educational system is usually defined as a failure to nurture talent. This includes failure to keep young people in the educational system and failure to do anything for them, even though they are kept in.

The identification of talent accents the notion that there is something there already, which, if we could just find it, would somehow serve us well. This has been the accent ever since the Sputniks, and even before that. It holds for finding assistant professors as well as for finding "qualified" freshmen. I have been amused as well as distressed to see committees who were searching for an assistant professor go on the assumption that somewhere, some place, they would find one who would perform admirably regardless of how he was treated after he was hired. This assumption involves the notion that somehow or another, everything a man needs for great achievement has already been built into him, and we need only to find that. I am saying that a man's performance as an assistant professor depends heavily on the kind of environment in which he functions.

This general philosophy of built-in abilities stems from the deeply based American conviction that everything worthwhile is scarce; that accordingly, education is scarce, and we must therefore find some system for determining who should get what. In education, of course, we cling to the merit system as a means for deciding who gets the best or the most advantageous kind of education.

The talent search activity of the last fifteen or twenty years has served to accent motivational and personality factors in addition to ability. The latter are, in fact, predictive of good performance in college, graduate school, and thereafter. I do not want, however, to over-accent the element of fixity in a person at the time he arrives at college or graduate school. I prefer to say, as I believe, that he still can develop. We ought not make our judgments primarily on the basis of what he is likely to do, by virtue of what he is already, but rather on the basis of what he might do, given a continuing good environment and a continuing opportunity.

If William James's career had been determined by today's standards, he would have been an artist. Or else everybody would have been terribly distressed when he dropped out of art school. As it happened, he was able to go on to various other schools, including a medical school, and eventually wound up as a philosopher. I think he was a better philosopher for having been first an artist, then a physician and physiological researcher, and then a psychologist. Therefore, I am in favor of keeping the options open, even right through college.

Then there is the dropping-out phenomenon, on which I can touch only briefly. Leaving college is a familiar problem to us all. While it is a complicated matter, it is not always a catastrophe or even an occasion for talent loss. Probably most of you are familiar with the work of Heist (1968), in which he pointed out that at five of the seven colleges he studied intensively, more potentially highly creative students dropped out than did regular students; in the two other colleges, the dropout rate was about the same for the two groups. He was talking here about rates of dropouts ranging from about 50 to 80 per cent. His underlying notion, I think, was that the more creative students could not stand the regime, the law and order of the traditional colleges. But it is clear, also, that the far-out colleges do not retain Heist's type of potentially creative students, either. If you take a college like Reed, where the typical freshman is very much like Heist's potentially creative student, the dropout rate among freshmen is also very high, though probably for quite different reasons. I think that in these latter cases, the students' impulses get so loose that no means of control can be found; as a result, the students cannot stand even a minimal structure.

As I said, dropping out of college is not catastrophic for the talented person, as we know from the work of MacKinnon (1962), who found that some of the most creative architects never even finished college. We do not have to go back many years to find extraordinarily creative people, like Arthur Morgan, who did not go to college at all, except late in his career and on a part-time basis. In fact, not going to college probably helped Morgan to be a whole man, instead of being overly specialized as so many of us become today.

Little is known, as far as I know, about the later careers of people who drop out of a particular college. Most, we know, go to some other college. How dropping out altogether affects their future careers is, as far as I know, quite obscure. Nowadays, of course, we have to deal with students who are not adapting very well to our tried-and-true educational methods. They are not only dropping out of the system and trying totally different kinds of systems; they are modifying quite radically the systems we have. A whole new look in pedagogy is confronting us right now, and it will be very interesting to see what happens in the future. This pedagogy is designed mainly for students who have found themselves frustrated by the usual academic regime. In any case, I would say that students who are finding it hard to adapt to the requirements of traditional higher educational institutions will probably be quite superior, in time, as long as their parents have faith in them and enough money to permit them to try this and that before they finally settle down. So we might turn out some William Jameses yet, if this faith and support can be maintained.

Loss of talent within the educational process itself should once again be accented. Here I am referring to the failure to develop the potential of students who stay in college. As we know, many, many students are hardly touched by four years of college, and a great many more drop out psychologically without actually leaving the campus. Volumes have been written about this, and more volumes need to be written, because this really is the key problem of higher education.

Here I limit my comments to some observations of what seems to go wrong. Some students become disillusioned early because they find that people they have admired have feet of clay, fail to find any adult model that seems remotely suitable, or become aware of the enormous corruption of the system to which they are asked to adapt themselves. Other students suffer almost irreparably from damage to self-esteem when, as freshmen, they are confronted with too much senseless competition at a time when talents are just beginning to emerge. Other students are lost because of a lack of challenge: nothing happens to appeal to their higher aspirations. This may result from desultory teaching, or from a desiccated curriculum which, in fact, does not connect with anything genuinely important.

Today, some are lost because of what might be called premature liberation of impulses. In other words, students who have had all the experiences there are by the time they get to college are no longer able to control their impulses. Since more than enough impulse gratification can be had all the time, why delay in order to learn anything? This is becoming, I think, a fairly serious problem.

The main trouble is that professors, by and large, are not really interested in education. They are interested in teaching subjects to students who hope to become professionals. They have no general theory of education, and very little knowledge about students. Radical changes, in my view, are quite necessary in order to cut down on the loss that occurs within the college system.

No one seems to know very much about failures in graduate school: their frequency is so great that no university will tell you, if it can help it, how many of their graduate students drop out. This is a very serious matter because the investment in those students at the time they drop out has already been heavy. But everybody knows they drop out; they are here today and gone tomorrow. Many of them simply do not connect with graduate school. They find nobody to talk to, for no professor has time for them. Others are extremely frustrated by the narrowness of the requirements, and they learn early in the game that they are not going to have a chance to gratify their curiosity. Many of them feel restrained by an overemphasis on narrow departmental requirements, and they are penalized if they look into another department to see what is going on there.

Nevertheless, it seems fair to say that in this society we hear few complaints about our failure to produce engineers, managers, physicians, psychologists, and so on; most people seem to look favorably upon the procedures by which this is done. They get upset only when faced with disruptions of the established training processes, or perhaps by apparent threats to the interests of those who are maintaining the existing system.

In short, I do not believe many people would argue that we are short of the talent needed to perform the most agreed tasks in our society; talent that is wasted is considered superfluous. Parents, by and large, are not complaining about this, because they have been brought up to believe the notion that if their children work hard enough, and deserve it, they will somehow somewhere find a place in the system, and will be suitably rewarded. Further, it is believed that people who do not find a place in the system really do not deserve it.

The real shortage in our society is a shortage of leaders. A shortage of people who can tell what kinds of experts we should produce, and what these experts ought to be doing. You cannot produce people like this by virtue of any kind of training. This can be effectively accomplished only through education, and education is not primarily a means for meeting manpower needs. In fact, many suitable candidates for the role of leader—of decision-maker in our society—are lost to the various specialties, where they can easily get quite suitable rewards. But I would say that if we had such people and if they were, in fact, allowed to lead us in building a society in which human needs came first, then present major causes of talent loss would be eradicated; in fact, various kinds of new professions would be developed, and all of the activities directly concerned with human development and well-being would be vastly expanded. For there is no end to what can be undertaken in the realm of what is distinctively human: in teaching, caring for people psychologically, learning artistic production and appreciation, and so on. Such a change in society, I think, is not out of the question.

I mentioned earlier how after World War II there was a big swing in the direction of mental health. And a swing in the direction I am indicating here is definitely the direction in which the new breed of young people is heading and wants the rest of us to go.

Education and training, in the society we may thus envision, would both be humanistic, that is, based on an understanding of what people are by nature, and of what they need to develop all their talent potential. Thus, we would direct our attention to a whole range of talents which are neglected in school or which are focused on the narrowly cognitive aspects of development. I am referring to talents such as those involved in communication, relating to people, perceptual clarity, and so on. If we implemented such a program, I believe many people now labeled disadvantaged would actually have advantages; particularly lower-class blacks who, when seen on college campuses today, turn out to be extraordinarily gifted communicators. It is too bad we do not have some here, because often in meetings of this kind, they are the only people present who can speak with passion without losing their heads. We can speak without losing our heads, but we have difficulty in being really passionate about it.

Of course, in this new kind of society new institutions would be established. In fact, they are being established now. For example, William Soskin, of the Psychological Clinic at the University of California, Berkeley, runs an after-school program for 300 high school youngsters from Berkeley. While it started out as a program for youngsters who had some problems about drugs, it has become in fact a personality developing institution. (They do not like to call it a school.) Everything that is done there contributes in some way to the overall development of the participants. Soskin says that he has had to give up trying to introduce this program into the regular school system, and that the only remaining option was to build an outside institution. This he has done. Since 80 per cent of the parents involved take part in evening programs at this same institution he believes that they will actively support it.

When attention is thus given to the development of the whole person, psychological testing will have to change in emphasis and direction; many human characteristics now given scant attention will become the objects of measurement. For example, we will ask of a given student how authoritarian he is, how rapidly he is getting over his authoritarianism, or what stage of ego-development he has reached. In other words, the accent will be upon what is needed now, in order to assist in the further development of the individual student.

Commentary

Nevitt Sanford

I see nothing wrong with having undergraduate colleges in universities and I glory in the fact that we have such a diversity of undergraduate institutions in this country—and we need many more. After all, we are trying today to carry on something like universal higher education with the use of an institution that is medieval, fundamentally, and in a way it has not changed in its basic structure since medieval times. Something's got to give, you know, and it is giving. What I would like to see is a whole range of new kinds of institutions designed to meet the needs of the individuals, improving but not tampering too much with the training programs which the universities have.

We are continuing to act as if this college, brought over from the middle ages, somehow is going to do the whole job. We have to think imaginatively and radically about the kinds of things that could be done. Books have been written of the kinds of things that can be done by way of changing the colleges—but the kinds of things that could be done in quite different sorts of institutions— all that is ahead of us.

This will mean that we will have to have some teachers. We have to have a whole new profession who are primarily teachers of individuals, who do not identify themselves primarily with an academic specialty—but who define themselves as teachers of the young. And I am hoping that this current generation of students will produce a whole new population of teachers of that kind.

Donald P. Hoyt

People really are different. One of the great shortcomings of education is to conceive of the well-rounded individual as the epitome of success. The sense of identity and uniqueness so basic to fundamental self-esteem seems to emerge more from a type of lopsidedness—the ways in which an individual is different from everyone else. Further development occurring in educational settings depends more on what the learner does than on what his teachers do, a concept quite difficult for faculty members to accept.

Leonard L. Baird

We at ACT have found that the flow of talent to colleges jobs, and schools is primarily related to academic talent and not to other sorts of talent, in such areas as art, music, writing, leadership, or even in science. The labeling of people who do not attend college as untalented, or less talented, is grossly misleading if you take this broad view of human talent. There is little lost talent. Talent goes somewhere that it can be used. Most, if not all, studies of talented persons use college graduate populations as if they were the only pool of talent. ACT's research results indicate that talented people can be found in many other kinds of groups.

Lyle D. Edmison

In an ideal society human talents and manpower problems can be found going together. However, this is an ideal, an objective toward which we work and by no means realized at the present time. We decry the widespread belief that talent development at public expense must seemingly be related to national purposes.

PART TWO

STUDENT
NEEDS

Robert S. Powell, Jr.

More Than
a Number

5

Some important decisions will have to be made in the next few years on our campuses. I think it is no surprise, particularly to those who are on the campus, when I say our system of higher education is in very deep trouble today.

The thrust of my remarks is not simply on the question of the student as a number and the desire to be more than that. I would be doing a disservice thus to limit my remarks. But I do want to discuss in some detail what is going on around the country in relationship to higher education, and try to offer some insights into the kinds of problems that the universities are facing.

To many Americans our self-esteem as a nation has rested on material affluence and our ability as a nation to produce goods and services more than any other nation in history. Indeed, for many of the generation who fought the battles of depression—and they were heavy battles—our material affluence is really a mark of our success as a nation. It is ample testimony toward the viability of our institutions. In the last few years, the federal government, in response, has returned much of that affluence to our campuses in the form of federal aid. We are now building vast new universities, more buildings, more research grants, and providing higher salaries for professors, along with more scholarships for students. Indeed our universities are prospering materially as they have never prospered before. And yet for students, our day-to-day experience indicates that the kind of education we are getting is frustrating, hollow, and devoid of the kinds of experiences we think we are going to need to make this country continue along the path of prosperity and spiritual leadership in the world that we think it needs.

If we can learn from the turmoil that is now racking our campuses, we could understand that millions of middle-class young people, who have shared rather richly in that hard-won affluence, not only do not prize that affluence, but consider it a positive handicap in the search for personal development and national integrity. The black and brown populations of our colleges and universities who, because of the operational racism in our economic, political, and educational institutions, have been systematically denied any of the benefits of those institutions, are angry. They are angry because they have been frauded, cheated, and ignored by those who make higher education policy. The only doors open, even to a small percentage of black and brown students these days, lead them to grossly inadequate, white-dominated, segregated institutions, mostly in the South. Those students are now saying, in long-overdue tones of anger, I think that we must do better as a nation.

Look around the country; some of the things going on are

deeply disturbing, despite the gross national product figures. The country's finding some of its most loyal and courageous young men choosing to go to jail, rather than bear their country's arms in service in Vietnam. Just last week the National Student Association released a petition signed by 250 student body presidents and campus editors, declaring that they would refuse induction and go to jail, rather than serve in the armed forces.

The drug scene is equally disturbing. In one ten-week period last fall, according to our clipping service at the association, over 16,000 college students were arrested for some form of drug abuse. Now, for one ten-week period, that is an alarming figure. More than 200 campuses have had demonstrations that required the police to come in and arrest students this year.

While some see all of this as an expression of student power, my analysis is much different. I see these events as an expression of student powerlessness. University officials, as well as political leaders, are expressing shock and anger that students would do such things as disrupt the university, which they say is trying to carry on free and open inquiry. The university, they say, and we are told, should teach people that persuasion is the technique and tool one uses in this society in order to get your demands achieved. Let us be quite honest for a moment. Does persuasion work in a university? Can a student, or a group of students, achieve significant changes that most people agree are necessary in the university, by use of persuasion, dialogue, and discourse? Or, have university officials responded only to disruptive and discordant student power tactics that lay the university open to the kind of divisiveness that we have seen all around the country this year?

To me the answer to that question is clear. Persuasion has not worked in the university, and those of us that have been pushing for nonviolent tactics and persuasion for many years on the campus are now finding university officials not backing us up with their actions, because they do not respond to persuasion. They do respond to violence.

The question of student power tactics is one I hope will continue to be the subject of debate for many years to come. Personally, I could not support those kinds of student power tactics that deny other students access to buildings or recruiters, which destroy property, or which harm other individuals on the campus physically. But I think we must be clear about where we put the responsibility for that kind of activity, and I for one, even though I would not support those kinds of activity, would have to place the responsibility for what is happening on our campuses squarely on the shoulders of the university, which is teaching powerlessness to young people in this country. I blame our universities for creating one of the most undemocratic institutions through which young people have to pass in order to achieve an educated adulthood.

There can be no persuasion, there can be no conversation as the current language goes, when students have no effective voice in the government of the university. I think we all know how decisions get made, and that two students on a big faculty committee do not always constitute an effective voice. Hence, I am not the least bit surprised that students are rejecting dialogue, so to speak, in favor of more direct action tactics. University administrators have demonstrated in the past few years that dialogue and persuasion are, by and large, a fruitless exercise, and the only agent of change left to utilize is direct action.

Let me explore this a bit further. In a very widely heralded letter of February 24 to President Hesburgh of Notre Dame, President Nixon struck what I think is a common theme around the country when he said this: "A fundamental governing principle of any great university is that the rule of reason and not the rule of force should prevail. Whoever rejects that principle," the President said, "forfeits his right to be a member of the academic community."

I would agree with that statement but the tragic irony of it, in my judgment, is that it was directed at the wrong constituency within the university. That admonition should have gone to administrators and faculty members, and not the students, because the university, sadly, is not now operating on the rule of reason, but on the rule of force, which the President and so many others including myself have so often deplored; and it is the rule of force that is the governing standard of most colleges and universities today. For example, the grading system, which is based primarily on the fear of failure and subsequent forcible expulsion from the university, forces students to conform to a system of education for which there are no alternatives at the present time. Few students would expend any energy in the courses the university requires them to take without the current grading system. If it were not for the frequent and often angry warnings of our federal courts, many university officials would still be forcibly expelling students on misconduct charges, without even the trappings of a fair hearing to allow the student to defend himself against the charges.

And what about policy-making over all? Here the rule of reason is most perverted, in my judgment. In most institutions, administrators, with the help of the faculty—the senior faculty—occasionally make sweeping and major policy decisions affecting the material and educational well-being of the students without ever involving the students. When the students respond with natural hostility, not only at the decision itself, but at the process of the decision, those with the power will listen carefully, and then do nothing. In total frustration and anger the students will call a demonstration. At this point, the administrators generally do act, by calling the police to forcibly break up the demonstration and enforce their original decision. That, to me, is not the rule of reason I learned to respect. And what it has shown me is that there is no particular reason for us to assume that the American academic and American university personnel are any more devoted to freedom and the rule of reason than American lawyers, businessmen, doctors, or welfare recipients. In fact, the last few years in higher education have demonstrated to the contrary, that the university may well be a mirror image of our deeply violent and coercive culture, and that those charged with its governance will employ censorship, the use of the police, expulsion, paid secret informants, and harsh and often unfair economic sanctions to enforce their version of a consensus on the citizens of their community.

It seems to me that is the fundamental problem we are facing when we talk about students and what they want. The kinds of things students are asking for today goes to the very heart of the principles on which this country was founded. That is the rule of reason, and the establishment of democratic institutions that are capable of responding to needs of its citizens. One of the most disturbing kinds of discussions going on today has to do with uses of the university.

Let us consider the uses of the university, and the way in which students want to play a part in that. One of the charges made at student activists these days is that they are making the university political. The university should not be a political institution, they say, it should be a place where quiet, thoughtful, scholarly pursuits go on, free from the kind of chaotic world view that has racked so many other institutions in our country.

I reject that on two counts. First, the university should be political; second, we ought to be honest with ourselves and admit that it has been political for a number of years. And what is happening now is that students are beginning to say, "We want to change the politics of that institution, from one set of politics to another."

Let me be specific. Our defense department and defense establishment could not survive a month were it not for the willing and thoughtful cooperation of our universities, which are providing the defense establishment with most of the research that is needed in order to conduct its affairs abroad. Millions, I should say billions, of dollars a year are poured into our universities from the defense department to promote the kind of research that leads us into Vietnam, the ABM, nuclear strategies, and all the other things that many of us find so abhorrent to foreign policy in this country. Many of us lived through the recent crisis with the selective service system, when General Hershey, several months ago, asked all the universities to dutifully rank its students so that he could know which ones to draft. And most of the universities complied willingly.

Consider urban universities, and the effect they have on the urban problems of the surrounding area. With policies that are thoughtless, at best, they mindlessly expand into the community, displacing thousands of people in housing that is inadequate. When the educational problems of the black community were becoming worse, what was happening in our universities? Admissions requirements were becoming more and more biased to white students with high test scores. Civil liberties on campus have often been, at best, raked by the administration at a time in which the right-wing people in this country are cracking down so hard on academic freedom. The response of the university in many cases is to crack down similarly on the political expression and the political freedom of its students.

I do not mind that the university is political. It should be political. It should not be an institution separate from our other institutions and the other problems this society faces. The university should nourish our culture, not retard it. The problem today is that the political values of the university are of the old order. Students are saying that the university should begin to nourish our culture rather than retard it; by working for peace, not for war; by beginning to provide some hope and some educational benefits to the black and brown community of our country, which has been denied those benefits systematically by other institutions; the university should cherish and nourish in students a love for civil liberties, self-government, and responsibility. It is not doing those things now. It stifles that kind of initiative by embodying the welfare state in its most corrupt form, in my judgment. We will do everything for you, the university says. You do not have to think for yourself, it tells its students.

Let me go, then, to a solution to some of these problems. Today's students have begun to develop some programs and some strategies for university change that can begin to turn around the direction in which the university is heading now. If we are to understand how we are to change the university, let me try to summarize what I have said. We are going to have to understand what is basically wrong.

In my judgment, the thing that is basically wrong is the way the government's procedure and the decision-making processes are set up at the present time. The basic governing principle at the university should be a democratic governing procedure, not an authoritarian one as the situation now is: *the rule of reason should prevail, not the rule of force.* And I think there are several things we should do to our universities if we want to put that principle into practice, the principle of democracy.

The first thing we are going to have to do is restrain the faculty. Those of us that have been fighting student power battles for many years often mistakenly saw the administration as the key problem in any significant university reform. I think most students who are into those battles now are beginning to see the problem goes much beyond the administration. The real changes that have to take place in university governance and university decisions are going to involve the faculty. The first thing that will have to be done, in my judgment, to restrain the faculty and give the students a much stronger voice in university decision, is to abolish the current grading system. This system only arms the faculty with the kinds of weapons it needs to keep the students in their place. The current grading system is based on fear and coercion. It is not based on sound educational principles, as most of the studies have demonstrated. It is, in fact, the central instrument of coercion in the university.

One of the results of the pass-fail grading systems that have been instituted around the country is that when the grade is removed from a class, the contact between professor and student is diminished. The interest in the subject matter is diminished. Nobody much cares any more when that grade is removed, because what was being done in the name of education was being done primarily because that grade was there. The students were coming to class because they would flunk if they did not. The professor was coming to class and preparing notes because he had to give a grade at the end of that course. The other motivations we thought were present in the educational process just are not there in too many cases—which tells me something very significant about the use of grades in the university. I think they should be abolished, and I think we should look for more sound methods of evaluating academic progress. Evaluation is terribly important, but the grading system is not the way to do it. I think most of us are fooling ourselves if

Robert S. Powell, Jr.

we think we are adequately evaluating the student's performance through the use of the current grading system.

The second problem of the faculty, other than the fact that it uses grades in this manner, is that the faculty in many cases brings to the educational process an elitism that I find rather dangerous. Most faculty members that one talks to have the sense that their own teaching profession, and particularly their subject matter, is defined by a statement something like the following: "That which I am teaching has an inherent worth far above and beyond any effect it has on the students I'm teaching." That kind of elitism goes into the building of a curriculum. The faculty makes the curriculum primarily to create more faculty members. When you look at the catalogue in the college, you find the curriculum set up to create political science professors, botany professors, and a lot of other professors, with often very little in the curriculum designed somehow to change the attitude of the students or to make for them a somewhat better life.

I think the students are going to have to participate in the building of that curriculum, because if it has no effect on the students, it is worthless. It has no inherent worth, other than what it does to the student, and the faculty should admit that. If they want to do their research, they should do their research and call it that, but they should not do it in the name of teaching.

And yet there is a third problem with the faculty, that, again, I think is beginning to be exposed, and overcome in many universities. And that is, that the faculty, for many years, was regarded as the expert in the field of education. That was a very great misconception on most people's part. Most faculty members are experts; no one would challenge that. They are experts in their field, but very few faculty members know the first thing about education, educational theory, and how learning takes place. How many faculty members have really gone through serious courses in educational theory? How many know something about the dynamics of learning? And how many can go into a classroom and conduct a stimulating session with students apart from a lecture on his own specific topic?

79

Expertise is something that has to be faced rather candidly in the university, and the candid admission, I would suggest, is that no one in the university is an expert about educational theory, and particularly learning theory. But the group that has the most to provide for that discussion is the students, because they are the ones who have education directed at them. If education is affecting them, you should ask them and they should tell you. If it is not affecting them, then that should say something to you about the system.

That leads me to conclude that if we are significantly going to restructure our universities, in order to make the student more than a number, he will have to build himself into the university in a way that is healthy. He will have to take a significant share of the responsibility for making decisions. And I do not mean decisions about dormitories only. And I do not mean decisions about drinking policy only. I mean more—decisions about academic structure, about educational policies the university adopts.

How can this happen? Let me suggest some specific ways. First, in 1969, it makes no sense to continue to have required curricula. Required curricula in most universities is an anachronism that goes back to the twenties and thirties and the traditionalist view of education. What required curricula and general education did was remove the only defense students had against bad teaching: the elective principle, and the right to choose one's own teachers. With requirements, the teachers are protected from the votes of the students as to how well they are teaching. Most universities are quite capable of providing the breadth of subject matter to students that they need to get a general education. Required curriculum is a holdover from an earlier day in which teachers were not regarded as experts. I think today students ought to be allowed the choice of leaving a professor's class empty if he is a bad professor.

The second thing that should be provided, and in increasing numbers it is, is student-initiated courses. The faculty can initiate courses, often with a good deal of success. One of the things the last few years in higher education has shown is that students are also capable of initiating academically sound courses. A very good example of this is the Committee for Participant Education at Berkeley, set up after the Free Speech Movement, which is a mechanism for allowing students at Berkeley to initiate courses for credit. The mechanism is simple. The student, or a group of students, or a group of faculty members with students, draws up the syllabus. They present it to the board of students and faculty members, and if it is approved as educationally sound, credit is granted and the grading requirements are modified according to the wishes of people in the class. The key element in student-initiated courses is that students are involved in the study. They are interested in it because it is something they have initiated on their own, and with the help of faculty members, academic quality can be maintained with very little difficulty.

I think there is a third thing that needs to be done. In order to protect the university from bad teaching and from professors who are not up to date in relevance to the needs of students, the students are going to have to be let into the decision-making about the selection and promotion of professors. This is beginning to happen around the country, again, with some success, for example, at places like Bennington. The students have, you must understand, a unique thing to bring to the decision about a faculty member. The thing they have, which is unique, is their feedback about the effect of that faculty member on the students with whom he comes into contact. The presence of the faculty member in the university is not something that is inherently good, in my judgment. The presence of the faculty member is a reality because the students are there to learn something from him. At the point at which the students can not learn from him, when he is not being effective, that ought to go into the decision-making relevant to promoting him, giving him tenure, or hiring him in the first place. That should be done in conjunction with our faculty members.

Then the last thing needed to be done, in which faculty can share their skills with students, is the development of new methods of evaluating academic progress. We just do not know how to evaluate academic progress. The one thing we do know is that the grading system we now have is a rather poor indicator of academic achievement or self-development. A lot of experiments are being tried, but not with the verve needed; because we are pretty satisfied, in many cases, with the current grading system. And I think a major assault needs to be made on that question. How can we build, in our universities, humane and educationally sound methods of evaluating academic progress?

All these things seem to be aimed at one fundamental goal of our educational system, that is, the creation of independent citizens who know how to think for themselves. The central problem our higher education has today, it seems to me, is that it is not encouraging self-development. The techniques we have set up to train students for citizenship in this country are inadequate to the extent that they do not develop in our young people the capacity for self-government. It seems to me that nothing could be more important than the development of a young citizenry that can think for itself, make decisions on its own, and have that very crucial experience during its four years of higher education.

Commentary

Lowell Heiny

I grant that there are many things wrong with education, there are many thing wrong with our society; but there are many things that are right about it also, and I am not ready to discard the whole thing. The final answer has to be some sort of a compromise as is true in all situations. The students are perhaps not demanding too much in the long run, but they are expecting it to happen too rapidly. I think we in the schools, and representing the older generation, have been too reluctant to change and to adapt too. In our universities today we can see efforts in some faculty members to remain aloof from it all. Others try to anticipate even the most radical student demand so as to avoid confrontations. Worse, there are no efforts made to organize effective alternative groups of students. Most of all, many are so intimidated that they cave in even before students exercise any pressures. If the colleges and universities would feel more sure about themselves, take a determined stand against any intimidation but inviting reasonable nonviolent discussions about how things could be improved, then I believe student rebellions could be so reduced as no longer to threaten the universities.

Carl Varner

The most effective way that you undercut the support of the mass of students for the militants is to initiate and institute meaningful reform and changes; that you meet the legitimate aspirations and needs of students; that you prove to them that what we call "working through the system" can and will work. Because to tell you the truth many of us just do not think it can. I feel quite strongly that the voice that the students have in curriculum, at least with my personal experience, is almost nil. When it does exist, it's tokenism. I think the faculty tends very jealously and unjustifiably to guard this prerogative. On the academic side of the university let me cite an example. The student government during the past semester decided to initiate a program of teacher evaluation and make it public. The members of the faculty were disdainful and did not believe we could do it. When we told them we were going to publish it they were appalled. Then, at the same time they were glad to say, "Yes, we want effective teachers," "We want the students to evaluate instructors," "We want students to evaluate the courses." But, they were saying, "Only on our terms" and "Don't tell anybody what you have seen." The fact is that the masses of students *are* concerned and are very upset with a lot of the present methods used by society. The fact that only a few actually are willing to place their entire lives on the line and get thrown in jail to initiate change and reform does not mean that they do not have the legitimate sympathy of a large number of students. I do not think the student revolt, at least the sympathies with it and the support for it is confined to a few militants. I think it is a very mass, a very real movement.

Arthur E. Smith

Evaluation is inevitable. You cannot escape it. We are going to be evaluated. We are going to be judged. Many of us will be judged even after we have died. And all of us face the judgment of our God. Let's not throw the evaluation system out. Let's work with it, not destroy it and confuse it. What would you substitute for grades? Most of the responses in human behavior can be reduced to a yes-or-no situation, a "go" or a "no-go." You operate or you do not operate. In evaluation of the product, the student, we are coming to it too slowly. If we have no required curriculum, I am not sure students make the choices that produce excellence and accomplishment in things that are important. Should the university be more democratic? It is perhaps too democratic. What we need is action, or our inaction may kill us all. I would like society to present a list of non-negotiable demands to students. Some of these might be that society expects as a result of education that youth will contribute something to society. Secondly, a person must accept the consequences of his actions. You cannot escape it. And thirdly, that the rules, no matter what they are, must be the same for everyone.

David P. Campbell

The Right College

6

Any discussion of what students want these days is undertaken only by the most foolhardy. Any pronouncements about which college is best for which student must be made in almost total ignorance of what impact any college makes on any student; so the topic of this chapter is a real challenge and a relevant one, and we all know how important relevance is today.

One change students will want in the coming years is a change in the mechanisms that shift various kinds of students into various kinds of colleges. To the student's desire for change is now being added the growing realization among our professional community that our selection methods are having some harmful side effects. Is our concept of "the right college for the right student" still a useful one?

The matching mechanism that we have now essentially is that each institution tries to admit as many students as it can of the type that it finds easiest to educate. To express this in another way, the selection process for most colleges is designed to admit those students least likely to drop out. There is little concern for selecting those who need the education most, nor those who can—in some absolute sense—profit most from it.

The best way to get into a high-powered eastern college is to appear to have all of the attributes of a budding Oxford scholar; the best way to get into one of the service academies, which in their way are as selective as the Ivy League, is to appear to have the ramrod qualities of a future Chief of Staff; the best way to get into Cal Tech or MIT is to appear to have the fanatic scientific dedication of a future Nobel Prize winner. Whenever an institution has more applicants than openings, the faculty usually manages to sway admissions policy in the direction of admitting those students who most closely resemble the faculty.

There is much less concern among faculty members to modify the academic community to accommodate those who are having trouble there. When a faculty committee is shown information on some factor related to dropout rate, their first reaction is something like, "We should be using that in admissions, and keep out those low students who are likely to drop out." I do not claim that my experience is very broad, but I have seen this happen a few times and never once has anyone said, "I wonder how we can change the system to help more of those people through."

One notable exception to this is the athletic department where they are interested in modifying the student's environment so that he can succeed. Curiously, the faculty usually looks askance at the coaches for doing this even though their efforts are apparently successful; a report at Minnesota a few years ago reported that the graduation rate among athletes was higher than among nonathletes.

A typical faculty attitude on selection, and one which you will find more and more students quarreling with in the coming years, appeared recently in a letter to *Science* magazine. A member of the philosophy department of Denison University wrote, concerning graduate school selection,

> We should be concerned with selecting those individuals who will make significant contributions to their field. . . . If standardized tests would serve these various purposes, what is the objection to them? For my part, I would be willing to use the number of hairs on a student's head divided by his weight times his height if that were an effective predictor [Schagrin, 1969].

That is a fairly typical attitude among faculty members who have never thought much about selection techniques and their side effects, and it is patent nonsense. I can cite several criteria for selection that will increase the probability of selecting students who will make valuable contributions but that are all unacceptable criteria for selection or for matching students to colleges. If dramatic achievement among our students is our goal, we should admit only men—they clearly have more visible achievements than women. Of course, we would admit only whites and, in addition to race, we should give heavy emphasis to religion. Jews, Mormons, and Unitarians do better, on the average, than do Catholics, Lutherans, and Methodists, at least on such indices as per capita listings in *Who's Who*. Physical attributes are also important. On the average, tall people do better than short people, and, although I have never seen data to support this, I am sure that attractive people do better than plain ones. Birth order also has an impact; firstborn children score higher on achievement tests and do better in school than later-borns, and, incidentally, twins do poorer. And, although the data are inconclusive, it is probably best to be borne by a woman who is physically young, or as some have said, to have a mother who is "chronologically deprived." Yet I can hardly imagine that we would ask on an admission blank for the mother's age when the applicant was born. Students, indeed all of us, become furious when evaluated by such criteria, yet statistically they are clearly related to accomplishment.

The student's vocational choice is also important—some occupations do not lend themselves to public accomplishments, and institutions that want visible alumni should shy away from students with those career goals. Dentistry is one example, farming is another, accounting is yet another. Can you name even a single famous CPA? Any institution interested only in turning out graduates who will be recognized by others for their achievements ("contributions to their field") had better stick closely with students who are interested in science or the arts, for those are the alumni who receive the kudos.

A composite of the traits I have just listed suggests that in today's academic admissions world, the equivalent of being born with a silver spoon in one's mouth is to be a tall, white, firstborn, Unitarian male interested in science and the arts, and if a school wants to select only those who will become most visible as adults, those are all relevant selection criteria.

Yet they all have the taint of unfairness. Why should a student be rejected just because he is short? And to reject him because he is, say, a Baptist seems contrary to the Constitution. And rejecting him because he intends to be a farmer is even more parochial. Usually we do not use these unfair selection variables, at least directly, but because these factors all tend to be related, some unexpected trends can creep in. I think students are becoming more aware of some of the inherent unfairness in our procedures, and the next generation will be a good deal more active in questioning our methods and their side effects.

To document some of these side effects, let me show you some trends in one institution. These figures happen to come from Dartmouth College, but they are probably representative of what has happened at most of the highly selective schools. In 1952, Dartmouth began using a college entrance examination for admission purposes. Since then, this test has been used, along with high school class standing and other information, in the admissions process. Students' scores on this test have increased over fifteen

David P. Campbell

years by more than 100 points, a full standard deviation (Campbell, 1969). One-fourth of the classes of the early fifties fell below the lowest scoring students of today, and only half of those early classes would be admitted today.

Let me ask three questions about this procedure and its results. First, when one selects students in this manner, what impact does it have on other student characteristics? Second, from an educational standpoint, should an institution follow such a rigid selection procedure? Third, from an ethical standpoint, does a college or university have the right to restrict itself to the top of the ability distribution? This is a question students are asking.

The first question—what other characteristics of the student body are affected?—can be answered partially by the mean scores on the scales of the Strong Vocational Interest Blank (SVIB) for each of the Dartmouth classes; this inventory was not used in selection but was filled in by each student after he arrived on campus. The scores on the SVIB scales indicate the degree of agreement between the student's likes and dislikes, and the likes and dislikes of the men in the specified occupations. Recent classes are more interested in the sciences, both the hard sciences and the social sciences, than the earlier classes, and we know from the predictive studies using this inventory that a good many more of these more recent high scoring students will seek careers in these fields. Interest has also increased in the cultural-esthetic area and in the social service area.

The area with the greatest decrease has been the business occupations. Is it any wonder that the Dartmouth alumni are beginning to perceive a generation gap? Another area of decrease has been the outdoor–skilled-trades-oriented occupations.

The SVIB's Academic Achievement scale contains items that differentiate students who earn high grades from those who earn lower grades. The scores are moderately correlated, about .30, with grade point, and with the student's persistence in school. Those earning B.A.'s average about 50, M.A.'s 55, Ph.D.'s 60. Students who drop out average about 40, those who never enter, 25 or 30. The increase in scores on this scale has been roughly ten points, again a full standard deviation, over the fifteen years and demonstrates a clear but indirect effect of the selection policies. If we had data on other variables, I am sure we could show other trends traceable, indirectly, to the admissions decisions. The point here is that the selection procedure has changed the composition of the student body in ways of which the admissions committee is unaware.

The second question: From an educational standpoint, should an institution engage in these restrictive selection procedures? Any discussion here has to be almost pure speculation, for we know almost nothing about the effect our colleges have on their students, and to suggest that one selection system is better than another does little more than reveal one's biases—which I certainly intend to do here.

The research results that are becoming available (Feldman and Newcomb, 1969) suggest that one of the most important impacts an institution has on a student is the other students that he is surrounded with, in other words, peer pressure. If you want a person to think like an intellectual, then surround him with your definition of intellectuals; if you want to imbue a student with religious values, then surround him with other religious people; if you are running a medical school and want to turn out general practitioners who will return to out-state towns to practice, then have your classes dominated by those rustic individuals who value the slow tempo of the countryside, who enjoy hunting and fishing and other rural pleasures—which may be one explanation of why hardly any medical schools are turning out general practitioners these days.

In short, if an institution knows what kind of individual it wants to turn out, then the most effective way is to select freshmen as close to that model as possible, and let them work on each other as peers. If a faculty that they respect is available as models, that undoubtedly is facilitating, but the peers will still have more influence, simply because they have more hours together.

What happens at West Point is a good example. They aspire to turn out leaders, so what they do is to select the best leaders they can find among their applicants and admit them, and they do an excellent job of this; of a given entering West Point class, about 15 per cent have been student body presidents, over half have been athletic team captains, and another sizeable proportion have been newspaper editors, Boys' State delegates, or in similar leadership roles. These boys are then immersed in an atmosphere for four years where they are told that decisiveness and self-confidence are important, and they rate each other every year on these attributes— formalized peer pressure—and all this under the supervision of a faculty who have themselves come through this environment. The young officers who survive this are indeed capable of leading men.

The problem is that such systems may turn out individuals with such homogeneous qualities that they cannot fulfill the demands of society. I have already alluded to the problem of the medical schools; their selection techniques are now geared to admitting students who intend to specialize or become medical researchers (again, like the people who are selecting them) so the medical schools are having trouble providing a pool of general practitioners. Concerning West Point, there is no question in my mind that they, with their selection procedures and resultant peer culture, turn out second lieutenants decisive enough to lead platoons; I am less convinced that their system is the best one for producing generals thoughtful enough to advise presidents.

I do not like the concept of a homogeneous student body.

A boy who grows up in Grosse Point, Michigan, or Edina, Minnesota, or Atherton, California, then is educated at Harvard or Stanford, and finally takes graduate work at Michigan or Minnesota or Berkeley will probably have the best education this society is capable of producing, yet he will probably *never* in his lifetime spend an hour talking to a machinist, or a farmer, or a truck driver, or a small town grocer. Unless he happens to go through that heterogenizing (I do not know if that is a word, but I need the opposite of *homogenizing*) that heterogenizing institution, the U.S. Army, he will simply never know that a world exists where people have IQ's below 115.

If you do not feel any concern for the boy from Grosse Point, at least worry about the machinist and the farmer who could profit by the exposure to bright, sophisticated people.

In general, I am suspicious of all homogenizing educational institutions, and the greatest homogenizing influence of all is an overengineered selection procedure. The desire of current students to—the next four words are inevitable—"do their own thing" is a reaction against our intention to press them into our mold, however noble that mold might be.

Finally, the third question, what are the ethics of the kind of selection programs we have been running? There are at least two controversial issues here; the first one concerns the rights of the individual being rejected. Is there any inherent reason that a kid who is bright has a greater right to a Yale education than one who is not? The argument that the bright one will profit more from it is very hard to document. Give a mediocre student four years at Yale and he might gain—in an absolute sense—a great deal more than his brighter counterpart, who will likely do well no matter where he goes. The quandary over whether to give the best education to those who are already best prepared, or to those most in need of it, or to all equally is a tough one, and another instance of that classic puzzle, enunciated by John Gardner, of how to run a society that believes in the conflicting values, "All men are created equal" and "May the best man win." If all men are equal, then all should have an equal chance at Yale.

I do not know how this should be resolved, but I am sure of one thing—sooner or later, a student with a College Board score of 400 or an ACT score of 10 is going to sue Yale on the grounds that he was discriminated against in the admissions process. Such lawsuits have already occurred in the industrial world over job applications; we are bound to be next.

The second ethical issue is, for me, much easier to resolve; that is, the question of whether the high prestige institutions have the right to skim off the top of the ability dimension and leave the educational problems to others. I think not.

We are having a hassle in Minnesota right now with a steel

company that processes taconite, a low-grade iron ore, by removing the valuable mineral and dumping the rest, the tailings, some 55,000 tons daily, into Lake Superior, one of the world's largest pure water lakes. The company claims, because of economic and practical factors, that they cannot process these tailings in a more acceptable way. To me, the selection actions of educational institutions are analogous. We are saying that, because of economic and practical factors, we cannot educate those in the lower portion of the normal curve and we are skimming off the valuable resources because they are easier and more fun to teach, and leaving the tailings to others. The results are already obvious, and the tailings of our educational system will probably plague us long after we have cleaned up Lake Superior.

Those are the problems; now, what suggestions do I have for new ways of matching students with colleges?

First, I would emphasize that so little is known about the impact that colleges have on students that better data are desperately needed before wise decisions are possible. One of the most unfortunate aspects of the way we now operate is that virtually everything known about college students is based on admissions data—virtually nothing is known about the graduating seniors. To make reasonable decisions, we must know more about what we have done to them and how we have done it. To give a specific example—what a student learns at a university is probably far more influenced by what he does outside of class than by any classroom activity. Perhaps universities should be more concerned with maximizing the number of faculty-student-coffee-cup encounters than with the number of volumes in the library; yet while this is obvious to any casual observer, virtually nothing is known about the role of coffee as an educational facilitator. Such issues should be the next concern for institutions such as ACT, that is, to help us accumulate information to evaluate the impact of our educational programs.

Second, I think we should strive for diversity in our institutions, both among the faculty and the students. Diversity is at least as important as excellence, at least when the latter is as narrowly

93

defined as it is in most academic settings. Some place on every campus there should be room on the faculty and in the student body for some odd-ball people—card sharks, bowling champions, welders, square dance callers. Perhaps we should have a Department of Diversity where the faculty member's only claim is to be an idiot savant in some peculiar skill. (Some would say we already have an abundance.) There are many arguments for diversity, but the best one may be Darwin's finding that the species with the most variations is the one most likely to survive environmental stress.

The last suggestion I would make is that we allow for more randomness. Statisticians have learned that it is impossible to control for all possible biasing factors when selecting samples for an experiment, so they have adopted the technique of random selection to protect themselves from systematic errors. The same technique might be employed, at least in a small way, in the student-institution matching process. What would happen if, for example, Harvard had two application forms, the first being that now in use, which would be acted on as it is now, the second being a three-by-five card with the words, "I would like to study at Harvard next fall" with a place for the individual's signature, which would be his sole application action. From the 25,000 or so that would be received, Harvard could pick 100 randomly and admit them sight unseen.

Think what this would do for the character of the freshman class, for this is likely the only way that a 65-year-old grandfather could get in, or a recently paroled felon, or a Siberian peasant, or simply a likeable fellow from Sleepy Eye, Minnesota, who has no visible accomplishments in his seventeen years because he has spent most of it lying on his back in a meadow of clover, watching cloud formations slide by. We know there are imperfections in our selection techniques that we are not aware of—would it really be too much risk to abandon a few cases to chance?

Before I stop, I should emphasize that I am not recommending the abandonment of the selection machinery we now have —indeed, I would like to see it expanded to cover more characteristics of the students. And I would especially like to see more information collected from the student on his way through the institution. Only in that way will we really learn what we are doing to him, and only with such information can the student decide what he really wants.

Commentary

Tom G. Sexton

There are many institutions that are searching for a scientific method to determine what school or schools a particular student can best attend. The student must know himself as well as his college. And I am not sure that we at the college can help him very much until he gets into college. But the student must know how he will fit in an institution and how an institution will fit him. It is just as important to know yourself as to know your institution. The last Congress passed a "Truth in Lending" act for consumers. I think in the educational field we need a "Truth in Educational Policies" policy for the consumer, the student. Too many institutions are trying to offer more programs than they can adequately finance.

Joseph D. Boyd

The admissions counselors that I know have tried to face up to the need for flexible standards for certain people that have been denied education in the past. There is still a long way to go. But on a relative basis we have come a long way. I can cite some figures here in my state (Illinois). Last year we had only 5.7 Negro students per 100, this year collectively we have 7.1. This is progress, not nearly as much as some would like to see but I think it is evidence that there is flexibility. Many of these students do not meet that historic test score and high school rank standard that many of them thought was so important. One other bit of data belongs here. I have studied carefully the choices that our very high ability students in Illinois made twelve years ago. We took the same number of people of the same relatively high ability and studied what they wanted to make of themselves twelve years later. We found dramatic differences. I am not sure that we in education have sensed yet what this means in facilities, faculty, and instructional policies. Interest in majors in the field of education alone is up 5 per cent; social science is up 3 per cent; business and political science is up four per cent; agriculture was down; engineering was cut in half, from 24 per cent to 12 per cent; arts and humanities are down. These data come from 50,000 students, a rather sizable sample. With the very high-ability students 40 per cent generally want to go into the occupational choices working with people. Among these recent grant winners we have identified, the percentage was 55 per cent. I think it really represents their decision, as they sense injustice, to make of their life something that will correct it. They are making this choice. We also should highlight here the number of high-ability students who are undecided; twelve years ago less than 1 per cent, now 8 per cent. I think they are telling us quite a bit, and the students themselves are affecting what the colleges are doing. I endorse very much the point that we must be more prepared to tell about the impact that the colleges have upon the student. I have been in sessions where the black students have spoken. They have already identified the campuses that indeed welcome them and serve them, and those that have not. Diversity, if it is going to work, has to be followed with positive programs to receive black students or the whole idea will simply backfire. There will be hypocrisy unless you have the curriculum, the counselors, and the attitude that will make these people feel that the experience is really worthwhile.

David P. Campbell

Ted R. Robinson

Selection, I would think, is much more a mutual process, and more selection is going on among prospective students than perhaps we acknowledge.

We should have a better device for providing information to students to assist them in making this selection. It is a very complex operation. In the final analysis, I find it difficult though to defend a random system, particularly where we have programs and institutions that are limited in resources and facilities. I find it difficult to defend to a prospective student and his parents the refusal of admission simply because by some random process someone else has taken his place.

Theodore M. Nelson

Guidance and Relevance

7

The concept of guidance and relevance has certain intriguing qualities about it—so intriguing that I could fill the pages allotted to me just on the semantics. But that would be approaching the topic in the manner that I am, in a sense, attacking.

Now, let me attempt to be relevant. In the beginnings of this guidance movement, the era of Frank Parsons to be exact, there did not seem to be a great deal of "science" about this business of helping human beings to seek worthwhile goals, vocationally or personally. But, due to careful analytical progress, we overcame this, and now we are "scientific." But have we lost something?

As we have evolved into a profession of counselors, psychologists, guidance workers, student personnel administrators, and educators, we seem to be evolving into a pattern that is similar to one that the testing movement has experienced.

If you recall from the history of our "business," the testing movement came about as a result of demands by the military in World War I, with their need to select and place individuals on the basis of needed skills within the military service. Following the army alpha experiences, the testing movement developed to select individuals for colleges and curriculums, with the emphasis upon meeting two needs: the needs of the college and the demands of the society. And with the emphasis upon these two primary points, little emphasis was given to the needs of the individual.

True, our earlier college catalogues of the 1920s and 1930s made noble pronouncements concerning the goals of their institutions and even gave some lip service to the needs of the human beings. But in the final analysis, did they? When we listen to people discussing tests, we still pick up connotations that tests are devices that keep people from doing something or are used to select a few individuals for certain particularly lucrative spots—lucrative academically, socially, or financially. In this sense one could say the devices or tools of guidance seem to have been used to provide techniques, information for filling a position. Unfortunately, very often the position carries more weight than the person.

In the 1930s we saw some shifts in direction, at least as conceived by the authors of tests and guidance devices. During this era, the development of testing devices began to be used to assess rather than to keep out. The function of these tests, or assessment devices, was to assist the individual in terms of his educational development. But again, many of us in our profession twisted this use. The information—perhaps subconsciously, perhaps deliberately—began to be used to validate how good we were as educators or how much better our system was than that of someone else.

But this kind of thinking and misuse of the guidance devices has caught up with us. The consumers of our devices, the students, are in many instances saying, "Let's get relevant." Let's get relevant with the devices in education to meet general and individual human needs rather than institutional needs and institutional control. Guidance, like the authors or devisers of its tool, the test, has been equally concerned with its degree of relevance.

The responsibility for irrelevance does not appear necessarily to lie with the authors of tests, the researchers (theoretical or applied)', the philosophers, or even the textbook writers. Nor does it necessarily lie in the laps of our consumers, the students. It appears that the problem of guidance and relevance lies with the facilitators, the in-betweeners, the go-betweeners. These, of course, are the counselors, personnel workers, psychologists, and educators.

Briefly, I should like to raise some questions concerning our roles as appliers of guidance philosophies and techniques. For example, how do we feel, personally in our roles, whether we be counselors, psychologists, or educators? Is it much more comfortable to be wrapped in the security of academic tradition, with its hang-ups about selection of students, or of academic standards, which, incidentally, are often a cover-up for academic inadequacy? Or are we simply afraid of making waves? Do we sometimes become trapped with our own egos or ego gratification in terms of, "I am here to tell you what to do"; or can we break from this and assist a human being in finding alternatives rather than escapes from failure? Have we become caught up in the game of jurisdictionalisms through an inner need for personal power, or are we willing to take the risk of crossing a jurisdictional line to assist a human being and take the calculated risk of having our colleagues say, "It's none of your business"?

As counselors and psychologists, we have, I believe, hidden behind certain façades of confidentiality in order to perpetuate our image of professional status. Have we been honest with ourselves in recognizing our lack of expertise in areas that could be most useful to our clients? For example, do we shy away from reading research and attempting to translate it into application? Perhaps we even shy away from it for fear that in asking for assistance in interpreting research someone will think we are inadequate. Granted, much of our research writing is difficult for those of us who do not have a theoretical or research orientation. But if we feel this way, should we not demand of our authors or journal editors and our researchers that they "tell it like it is," in language we can understand?

Do we sneer at people who speak of data systems or student data banks as depersonalized monsters engulfing our society, or do we see, as C. Gilbert Wrenn of Macalester College so succinctly put in a recent speech to the counselors of Colorado, "That here are materials and techniques that can help us to be relevant and help our students realistically look at their talents and potentials?" I would raise this question particularly of my colleagues who now label themselves the humanistic psychologists. Some of us with this orientation have become so enamored with the concept of feeling and sensitivity that we have lost sight of a rather simple concept that one's life space, as well as one's self-concept, is essentially based on information and experiences. Of course, the more relevant the experiences, the more relevant the self.

For years journals and articles dealing with college dropouts and attrition rates have carried the phrase, "the normal attrition rate is . . . ," and we accept it at that, rather than question, "Why an attrition rate at all?" It is comfortable to accept a normal attrition rate, but if one digs just slightly deeper one discovers that attrition percentages are made up of human beings. True, the attrition rate can be interpreted as a change in goals, but I wonder if we really interpret it that way. If we do, perhaps it is a rationalization for something we have left undone.

These, I believe, are some of the phenomena that have been a part of making us irrelevant. What, then, are some of the approaches to relevance in this rapidly changing society on and off the campus?

I suggest we make use of devices that agencies such as ACT are producing to help us become relevant. For example, the pioneer work of Pace and Stern and their climate indexes are a most useful beginning for understanding our students as well as our colleagues.

Guidance profiles and Institutional Self-Study Surveys from ACT are excellent tools to assist us in becoming aware of the needs of individuals as well as the many subgroups that make up our educational institutions.

Again, the administration, scoring, and processing of these devices is of little use unless they are translated and communicated to those concerned. In a sense, I am suggesting making use of these available materials for local research to develop better local understandings.

Local research need not be supported with huge computers, sophisticated statisticians, or theoreticians. Meaningful local research can be as simple as going out across the campus or into a classroom and saying, "What do you think?" and then, of course, listening to it. It is evident from conversations of colleagues at conventions and meetings that it is more delightful to discuss personality theory, latest pronouncements of Carl Rogers, Abraham Maslow, and Erich Fromm than to get practical. Listen to your graduate students in psychology and counseling, and you will hear the same sort of discussions. Granted, that theory and conceptualization are necessary, but to translate our esoteric personal interest in theory into meaningful practices seems to threaten our scholarly egos. We have become so wrapped up in seeking hidden motives that we cannot face straightforward questions about whether to become an electrician or an electrician's helper.

As to research, we need more broad dimension research that relates to personality dynamics as they mesh with the realities of the world of work and living. Examples of this include the work of Donald Super, and the very recent and relevant work of Holland, Astin, and Munday are of this caliber. Our gestalt psychologists have pleaded for the study of the whole man, the life space. It seems that their pleas should be answered by more of this type of research. And again, may I underline that when the research is completed it be interpreted to those of us who are the appliers.

We need to make greater effort to cross professional jurisdictional barriers. We need to communicate across professional lines. We need vehicles for this type of activity; for example, guidance workshops should be expanded to include those people in industry, employment services, and other agencies committed to youth rather than close-knit professional meetings with dull papers that feed only the egos of the speakers.

This gives me an opportunity to encourage particular types of educational conferences. With some financial assistance from ACT, Colorado and Wyoming counselors had an opportunity to sit down with industrial personnel, employment service, and rehabilitation counselors to discuss living and working problems of youth. And I could cite several other examples. This cross-fertilization of the profession seemed an absolute necessity, for example, at the fall meeting of the National Association of University Counseling Center Directors. There were lengthy discussions, formal and informal, concerning the need for counselors to get out of their medical models, to get out among the students and academic colleagues, to develop an outreach concept of counseling. This too suggests a need to be in contact with others who deal with youth. Many of us have discovered that faculty members can be markedly interested in students when they understand what their needs are. Is this interpretation of needs one of our roles in personnel work and counseling? Is it one of our roles to serve with curriculum specialists and the academic faculty committees to discuss the needs of our students, as the students have interpreted them to us?

What of our present training programs in personnel work, counseling, and guidance? Are these programs so structured to meet requirements for certification that they do not allow for innovation and response to change? Have our graduate programs become too course-oriented, research-oriented, or perhaps even too process-oriented? Needless to say, all three are necessary; but they must be tied together with the overall objective of preparing our professionals for their primary responsibility—that of being sensitive, skilled, knowledgeable, confident helpers of human beings.

I suspect my plea is, in essence, to keep our theory and practice in constant communication, but also to keep theory and practice relevant to those we serve. Too often the minute you hang a Ph.D. or an Ed.D. on a graduate student, he loses the security of being practical and seeks the security of the ivory tower.

But the ivory tower was built upon a foundation, and this foundation is expected to support the tower. Perhaps the time has come, however, to climb down the stairs of our towers and go down into the basement and examine the foundation. It just might be that part of this foundation needs to be replaced or reinforced. And this may be very relevant.

Commentary

Elias Blake, Jr.

Our organization has been working for the last two years with Negro colleges trying to help them develop more relevant curriculum that is effective for their students. One of the big problems that the counselors talk about is questions about identity—a general question of "Who am I?" The young people are not only asking themselves these questions; they are also concerned with the worry, "If I am going to be educated, if I am going to do something, I had better make a contribution." There is a great deal of confusion about relationship to teachers, relationship to adults, relationship to the first outside employer, relationship to the whole industrial world outside of the institution.

Another area, the area of frustration and anger, hostility and control of aggression goes along with this. They find that a lot of the frustration, a lot of the anger comes out of the instructional process. Nobody ever gets around to trying to figure out any feedback system into the instructional process so that people become more sensitive to what they are doing to young people in their classrooms. When they hide behind their Ph.D.'s or other qualifications they avoid really dealing with a typical kind of question that the student might raise in the context of the classroom.

People who work with young people are really very weak on the whole business of popular culture. You find very few adults over the age of thirty who know anything about the popular culture within which young people are immersing themselves. From my own memory I just do not hear in the 1940 popular culture the kinds of things that I hear in the popular culture today. Music is the big thing. Music has always been important. But this particular music expresses a whole lot of other attitudes. This is a symptom of a whole way of looking at the world, of a whole way of trying to perceive one's environment and the meaning of that environment. It may not be necessary for us to understand the stand that a particular student takes. But I think it is necessary, at least on an intellectual level, to understand the logic of it. If you understand the logic of it, then maybe you can ask the student some of the important questions.

In terms of psychological services inside a college and university people need to ask themselves about the whole institutional climate inside institutions. The institutions have been naive not to assume that there were going to be serious problems in adjusting to large numbers of minority group people who have never functioned in any way inside the institution. A large institution has many secretaries, security people, cafeteria workers, all other kinds of functionaries who, with the faculty, make up the atmosphere within which these new students have to operate. And, naively, the faculty meets, makes up its mind, and feels that it has dealt with the major source of its problems. Faculty members are naive in the extreme since many of the triggering incidents which have brought on confrontations with black students have come out of nonacademic problems. In St. Louis a whole issue revolved around a security guard and what he said to a black student. The problem is that many young people simply do not respect the people with whom they have to deal because they cannot find out where they stand. As counselors we tend not to want to talk to students about their various kinds of worries. They may have to deal with difficult problems such as a certain confrontation against shabby kinds of practices and treatments of students on the college campus. Therefore, we do not really want to get into that. Is that a legitimate way for people to work with young people in a college or university environment? These are the kinds of things that all of us need to think about in dealing with young people. It is not easy and when it gets to the point where you cannot go any further, you simply have to say, "This is where I draw the line." But I have found that if they know where you stand it does not bother them even though, interesting enough, they know you disagree with a great many things they are doing.

Carl B. Wiemann, Jr.

Better communication and understanding is needed among the many kinds of people involved in helping others. What is needed is a broad definition of guidance. People other than student personnel workers—parents, teachers, friends, and many others—are trying to help other human beings. It is easy for people with a college education to forget that about 80 per cent of the adults in this country who are twenty-five years old and over have not attended college. Therefore, articles in professional journals, written for other professionals, are not a satisfactory answer to better communication. And better communication and understanding is needed when one person tries to help another person. Whether it be parent and child, guidance counselor and student, or psychologist and client, more emphasis could be placed on how *they* (the persons hopefully being helped) see themselves, how *they* see their future life, and what is relevant to *them*.

H. Kenneth Barker

When we talk about relevance, have we considered the fact that people preparing today in the field of guidance are going to be working ten years from now? Have we given any consideration in training today for relevance to the situations they are going to meet ten years from now? I am quite certain when we were educated nobody dreamed of the kind of problems we deal with today. We ought to build into our program at least some motion of dealing with situations that are still totally unknown.

Harold Taylor

Student
Unrest

8

Student unrest is only a small part of something bigger. The whole world is in a state of unrest, and the old authorities have given way, disintegrated, before new authorities have come into being. The world's state of unrest has no parallel in history, since never before has the world as a whole been so interconnected. One kind of unrest in one country—Berkeley in the United States—has an effect of another kind in another country—Nanterre in France. One of the reasons for the world's unrest lies in the simple fact that the world's communications system now allows so many of the global population to know what the rest of mankind is doing. Whole countries which in the past were in ignorance of political and social action elsewhere have now learned what the others are doing and how to get what they want through direct action, following the example of others.

It is a mistake to think of American student unrest as a phenomenon unconnected to world events—wars, riots, revolutions, and radical social change—or unconnected to the American past, both in education and society. The unrest was beginning in the 1950s at a time when we looked at the younger generation through the eyes of journalists and writers whose business it was to write, and thus to influence, contemporary history. The generation of the 1950s was labeled by journalists as the Silent Generation, to describe those young people who were not silent but who refused to speak publicly about their inner thoughts and were therefore falsely identified in the public mind as silent members of an affluent society.

But through the 1950s students were restive and quite articulate. They were talking among themselves, having realized that to speak to the older generation about its problems, its politics, and its attitudes was to get yourself into trouble. They spoke to themselves, and as they spoke together, Holden Caulfield, Franny Glass, and others, inside and outside the novels of Salinger, said devastating things about the dangers of the atomic bomb, about John Foster Dulles, about General Eisenhower, about the leadership of the country. Under the surface of the calm expressed by Eisenhower and others in his administration, there was an interesting and restive group which condemned the hypocrisy of the older generation. They wished to keep their thoughts to themselves, since if they expressed themselves publicly, in political terms, they were denounced and condemned by their elders. The younger generation wanted its own kind of trouble, and not the kind induced by the then-Senator McCarthy, or John Foster Dulles, or the nuclear age. It was an intelligent, sensitive generation, concerned with personal and internal values they held within the community of the colleges, the high schools, and private schools, making devastating criticisms about the leadership of contemporary America. In a sense, the father of the protest movement was J. D. Salinger. He wrote about those who cared for the quality of life, not for the success pattern of American society.

In those days, young people like Woody Allen were growing up. Woody Allen, who has expressed himself on educational questions from time to time, said that he went to a school for mentally disturbed teachers. He said that he flunked out of NYU for having cheated on his final examination in metaphysics. He was a philosophy student who, as he pointed out, studied Comparative Truth 102, Intermediate Truth 101, and God 103, and his cheating, he said, consisted in having stared into the soul of the student sitting next to him. He has also criticized the educational system of the 1950s, then under the influence of the Sputnik syndrome, on the grounds that everything went too fast and he kept being put into brighter groups, although he thought everyone in the group was brighter than he was. Everything was speeded up so fast that in the contemporary civilization course, he discovered that the class read *War and Peace* in twenty minutes. He was able to say, after his experience with the book, that it was a book about Russia. Woody Allen was a member of the internal community of students in the 1950s. He left to join the successful dropouts.

The lively, imaginative, and politically aware young people of the 1950s were not generally known to the journalists. They were looking for other stories. America was looking for something that could be advertised, publicized, and talked about, but neglected to note what was happening within the consciousness of the younger generation. As we moved into the latter years of the 1950s and the early years of the 1960s, before the eyes of the younger generation, the inequities and injustices of the American community were revealed by the public media of television, the news magazine, and the paperbacks. The civil rights movement began as a movement of young people. Although the older generation was in some degree conscious of the injustices, the older generation had not acted to correct them. With the Supreme Court decision in the early years of the 1950s, the younger generation received a new franchise—a legitimacy to action, subsidized, in a sense, by the application of the laws of the country to existing situations.

In the latter years of the 1950s, a new generation of young people came alive to the realities of social injustice in America by seeing before their eyes members of their own generation beaten by police, goaded by cattle prods, brutalized by attackers, jailed, and in some cases killed. This was advertised to us in national reports on television and in the mass media. In that point in time, a new attitude was generated within the younger generation and became part of contemporary history. A new generation, having been subsidized by the educational system and informed by the mass media about the reality of contemporary society, moved into an era in which many of the young knew more about their own society than did their elders. They grew up in an era in which there was no depression, no war, and no McCarthyism. They sprang full-blown into an era in American history in which, supported in comparative affluence by their parents, they went to colleges and schools where information was publicly available on the issues important to world society and to American society. One could make up one's own mind about injustice or justice, about reality or unreality.

During the time that my generation was in school and college, the public information available to us about what was happening in American and world society was relatively trivial. I can recall in my boyhood having listened to KDKA in Pittsburgh on a radio set which worked with a crystal and used earphones. We heard KDKA, Paul Whiteman, and occasional news reports. That was the extent of the mass media in the era in which I grew up. Whatever information was available for me and my contemporaries came to us from the schools and from the official information provided to us by the colleges.

But now the young have access to a wider world, and they have become morally outraged by what they have discovered about their own society and about world society. The three issues they came to learn about were the immorality of war, the immorality of racial injustice, and the unnecessary immorality of poverty. In youth of the white American middle class, a new spirit grew, fed by information from a white middle-class society through its mass media. As they became of age in the 1960s, they found their own situation in it. First, they discovered that as eighteen-, nineteen-, and twenty-year-olds, they had equal rights as citizens with every other American citizen. If they wished to organize politically on their campuses, it was their right as citizens to do so. Secondly, they discovered that they had a right to a good education, one not being provided by the mass, dehumanized programs of the big, American university. On these two points they organized a rebellion that achieved some success and which in the future will achieve more.

In that period the new generation achieved a new characterization—restive, energetic, imaginative, sophisticated, practical-minded, and, at the same time, idealistic. The generation had been prepared by the civil rights movement to take deliberate action in concrete circumstance about concrete social evils. As we look at the early 1960s as a particular point in American history, we find the thrust of the younger generation to have been a major force in drawing the attention of the American public to the situation of the American community at large. That is to say, the rights which the students were demanding at the University of California in Berkeley were rights which many other people were demanding elsewhere. Among them were the members of the black community, who had been deprived of an educational opportunity worthy of their possibilities. The black community began to achieve its own expectations for itself. Its members began to demand things which they had never demanded in previous years. They reached a point in their own history at which they realized that the deprivation of educational opportunity was a crucial factor in their future lives. As the civil rights movement grew, as Martin Luther King, with his philosophy of nonviolence, exerted more and more effect on the attitude of the white American public, a whole new movement grew in which the students began to involve themselves. The new restlessness, new attitudes, and new sophistication on the part of white American youth combined with the growing militancy of the black community toward the achievement of privileges hitherto denied to them provided a new force in American politics.

We now come to today, to a young man, nineteen years of age, James Kunen, who has just published a book (1968) which he calls *The Strawberry Statement: Notes of a College Revolutionary*. We find him to be a sophomore at Columbia University who is affected by the events of 1968 at Columbia. As a member of the rowing crew, a graduate of Andover, and a proper, young, white American with all the right credentials, he testifies to the fact that he was radicalized by the events in his own life at Columbia. The term *Strawberry Statement* comes from a remark of a dean at Columbia University who referred to student opinion as a question of whether or not students preferred strawberry or vanilla in their politics. Kunen says, in this book, "There are those who want an armed revolution, and I'm not one of them. Not just now. But I do have a statement to make at this time. Gentlemen, since the first republic of the United States is 192 years old, and I am nineteen, I will give it one more chance."

I cite this as one example of the spirit of this particular generation. "Isn't it singular that no one ever goes to jail for waging wars," says Kunen, "let alone for advocating them. But the jails are filled with those who want peace. Not to kill is to be a criminal; they put you into jail if all you do is ask them to leave you alone."

Kunen expresses, in his action, his thoughts, and his education, the spirit of a new generation that is cut away from the past. Unless we realize that, we do not really know what we are talking about. Kunen's generation is a tough-minded, uninhibited group of well-informed young people who refuse to accept the world as they find it. It is now possible to say there is a world student movement. It is a world revolution developed by the young, many of whom are students who have now become spokesmen for their society and for all those who in previous years had been held back by the political and social system in which their parents have been captured. The new young have sprung full-blown into a world they did not make and which they intend remaking. Around

113

the world this generation is not inhibited by the class attitudes its members are expected to take to the governing authorities. Around the world they take themselves and their place in society seriously. As the students congregate in the universities of the world, they find assembled there in their internal communities, persons with whom they share like interests in poetry, politics, the arts, literature, and social action.

They are a new class, free from the political inhibitions which have prevented generations from thinking freely about a classless society that could be formed on an international scale through the efforts of the young. They feel that such a society could be obtained by those who, if they joined together, could abolish war, could accomplish the fair distribution of the world's goods, and could create a kind of healing of the breach between the rich and the poor, the haves and the have-nots, the destitute and the affluent. In the absence of an international spirit of compassion, among the world's governments, the younger generation finds itself introduced to a world society which has become accustomed to running itself by force and violence. The rhetoric of hostility is the norm in the international vocabulary, and it is no longer customary to appeal to the principle of human rights or a deep concern for the welfare of all persons. Instead, the illusory power of coercion has been invoked to solve political problems. In Vietnam, in Nigeria, in the Middle East, in Czechoslovakia, in China, force is in the saddle.

The difficulty in finding solutions to the world's political problems is now compounded by the fact that millions more of the world's people are taking a direct part in asserting their claims to be heard where the decisions are made. Decisions used to be made in the colonial period, and in the earlier part of the twentieth century, by white elites, by small groups within nations, by political, military, and economic power held by a few countries and a few persons in those countries. Now, millions demand a share in the decision-making. Whites and nonwhites in every part of the world are making confrontations of every kind, in many cases led by students, to fulfill a new kind of expectation on the part of those who in former years were victims of oppression. These people have now declared their intention no longer to stay in that position. If no one else will speak for their rights, or take responsibility for their economic, social, and personal welfare, they will do it themselves. When we look at the actions of the world generation of youth from a new perspective, the present unrest in the communities of America becomes identical with that kind of unrest to be found in the communities of the world.

There is, therefore, a necessary and, in a sense, inevitable connection between the ideas and actions of the younger generation around the world and the ideas and actions of the American student protest movement. The protest movement is a form of international education, conducted by the younger generation against the political, economic, and social control of those in power. We owe to the Czech students and Polish students, to the young Indonesians, Japanese, Egyptians, and French, and even English art school students, a debt for their part in making the issues in human rights clearer to the societies in which they live.

During the 1950s and 1960s, while the educators and political leaders went about their business of governing and controlling, protected from the reality of the ideas and feelings of youth by an elite position in the society, an international community of world youth was forming itself deep within the collective unconscious of a new world culture. Without communication of a direct kind among themselves, the world's students have formed the expression of a new age. In their separate societies they have expressed in action what they shared in common without knowing it. The place where their expressions were found was the place they were assembled in large numbers by those who hoped to induct them into the present society. That is, in the university.

Carlos Romulo put the matter squarely in his address (1968) to the United Nations General Assembly at the twentieth anniversary celebration of the Universal Declaration of Human Rights in December of 1968. General Romulo, Foreign Minister for the Philippines and a former university president, referred to the "clamor and agitation of disaffected youth everywhere" as

115

having "dramatized the basic democratic right of dissent." But then Romulo went on to say something I found startling in a man whom I had always considered to be a conservative:

> By challenging the traditional values, this generation has compelled society and the state to accept, although with reluctance, the principle of the inevitable transformation of society. By invoking violence as a necessary tool or weapon in given situations, it seeks to speed up the pace of change through the adventurous spirit of innovation. The phenomenon of youth in rebellion is universal, respecting neither national or ideological frontiers. Aggressive and defiant, fired by a raging discontent with things as they are, this young, brash, and impatient generation is our best ally in the effort to fulfill the great promise of the Universal Declaration of Human Rights. But, we must try to discover the real sources of its discontent, for only then can society hope to harness its militant idealism to the goals of the common good.

Across the world the ideas and feelings of youth have gathered around three focal points. Around these points the American students have gathered along with their unseen colleagues and compatriots in other parts of the world. First, a refusal to accept any longer the social and intellectual control of those in the society who give them no part in making decisions about what that society should be. Secondly, a demand found in the universities of the world by the students that the obsolete university curriculum, controlled by the academic faculty and made in the interests of the faculty, be subject to drastic reform. I had the opportunity a little over a month ago to talk with some of the Italian students who had been occupying the buildings of the University of Rome. I was curious to discover by talking with them what they hoped to accomplish by occupying the buildings day after day. One would think that there were other things they might be doing if they wanted to change the university and to do something about their society and the world. I discovered in the conversation that they had lost interest in changing the university, since they thought it to be so far gone, so unapproachable by anything they could do, that it was impossible to change it. Therefore, they had decided to do everything they could to destroy it.

They organized themselves but refused to have student representatives elected to negotiate with the government and the university authorities. They felt the most important thing they could do for their community, for other students, and for anybody else in Italy, was to bring down the government, which they considered to be corrupt, decadent, and so weak as to be unable to handle the problems of Italy. The faculty, I discovered, had little interest in changing the university. They were about to call a strike in order to defend their archaic rights of control and of lecturing once every two weeks and paying no attention to the students. I met with one professor, a distinguished professor of international law, who had risen at five in the morning and flown all the way from Geneva in order to give a nine o'clock lecture. He found himself accosted at the gates of the university. The students asked him his name, which he gave. They decided, after checking him off the list, that he was not a person from whom they wished to learn. He was very disappointed, having flown all the way from Geneva, not to be able to deliver his lecture.

Here was a group of students who were using the university as an institutional base through which they hoped to be able to organize a mass movement against the Italian government, against capitalism and the present system of Italian politics. They wanted to form a new, one-party system in which the students and the workers would form a new community with political power.

They considered the Communist party a reactionary political machine hitched up to the Italian government. Attitudes similar to these are to be found among a few people in the United States who are organized on the campuses in order to do damage to the university. They hope that by damaging the university, they will bring down the American system of government and the political system under which we all operate. They form a small section of the radical student movement, and factually, a relatively small element of the radical student movement is in control of or informed by those who would agree with the Italian students. But the demand for the reform of an obsolete university curriculum is one which is to be found all around the world, from Japan to Indonesia, to the African universities, to Poland, to Czechoslovakia, to America.

The third rallying point of the world generation of contemporary youth is a philosophy of radical subjectivism. That is to say, a radical assertion of the freedom to think, to speak, to act, to learn, to invest oneself in a new kind of life which opens up the future, refuses the official culture, and refuses to accept whatever is accepted. This is derived as the right of youth and the central value animating political and social change. Some of this was expressed by the French students in 1968, in their revolt against the French government and French society, when they painted their slogans on the walls: "I decree a state of happiness." "When a finger points at the moon, an imbecile looks at the finger." "Forbid all forbidding." "Be realistic—demand the impossible." "Poetry is in the streets." "Culture is the inversion of life."

It was a twenty-three-year-old sociology student from the University of Nanterre who, in the spontaneous uprising of 1968, managed to mobilize a whole sector of the French student body into political action, which, had it gone on with more astute leadership, might very well have brought down de Gaulle's government. One can argue now that Cohn-Bendit and the students have succeeded, since de Gaulle has since been retired. However, I think even Cohn-Bendit would not claim it was entirely his doing, although he just might—he has a great deal of radical subjectivism in him.

Within the new generation we have the creation of a new kind of leadership—a kind we may or may not like. In 1964, it was the twenty-four-year-old philosophy major, Mario Savio, at the University of California, who when he rose to make his eloquent statement on the roof of a police car containing a graduate student of mathematics, electrified 6,000 students and started a new movement so powerful that when in those days he chose to speak in public about his educational, political, and social views, 300–400 television, radio, and press reporters gathered around him.

118

Harold Taylor

We must also take note that later a twenty-four-year-old graduate of Howard University and an officer of a small organization of blacks, Stokely Carmichael, in a very short time after taking office was listened to seriously by a large American and international audience.

The younger generation has thus created its own leaders. When the question is raised about how the younger generation or any other generation can produce change in the society, what this younger generation wants, or how the young can work at the problem of their own society, there is a set of answers made by the very conditions in which the young are now enmeshed. As Kunen says, with the wisdom of a nineteen-year-old, "There are those who want an armed revolution. And I am not one of them. Not just now." Kunen is white, has had the privileges of a white, affluent society, including an opportunity for education of a kind which, at Columbia, he considers inadequate on any justifiable grounds, but nevertheless, an education. The members of Kunen's age group who are poor and black, brown, or white, do not have the powerful instruments of his wit or the literary style, or his access to the public media in order to press their case. But Kunen and others like him are pressing the case of the others, since they have an audience in the mass media and can be heard.

Within one sector of the black community there are those who say that black revolution is the only way to change the society and its educational system. In a very small sector of the white radical movement, there are those who agree with that principle, although they are not as prepared as some militant blacks for the theory that power comes from the barrel of a gun. Starting from that point, the question is: If power does not come from the barrel of a gun, then from where does power come for those who refuse to use guns?

Going back to the campus the question is: How does the student change society through his work at a university, when even the faculty remain uninterested in the society of which they are a part, detached from the interests of students, and aggrieved if asked to address itself as a collective body to the problems of reaching moral, political, and social decisions about the role of the university itself? That is what annoys, frustrates, and creates anger in the student body—that the faculty of the university itself will not face up to the issues which the young find so pressing. Among the more perceptive students, it soon becomes clear that submission on their part to the system of lectures, examinations, academic credits, grades, fraternities, sororities, and to the cultural sterility of the contemporary classroom, will lead only to a generalized state of numbed intellectual poverty. That is the considered judgment of those students who are astute enough to be conscious of their position.

What do you do, then, as a student, when you realize the education you are given is sterile, that the society is complacent, that the government can send you to war against people with whom you have no quarrel? If you do not do what you were told inside the academic system you will be pushed out to face a world in which academic credentials are a necessary condition for moving into any level of service that demands more than manual dexterity. Students as intelligent as Kunen, therefore, declare themselves to be revolutionaries. I must say in passing, that Kunen is a relatively harmless one who went on rowing in the crew at Columbia at the time the revolution there was taking place. His revolutionary acts were fitted into the time he could spare from other interests. Other students, with less grace and more revolutionary vigor, have planned tactics and strategies to shake the complacency of the universities and their surrounding societies. They are attacking the university in order to get at the society.

Since they cannot attack the society directly they are using the place they know best in order to achieve what results they can. This, to me, is the explanation of the extreme situation produced at Cornell University and at Harvard, where small groups of students have taken the bull by the horns, occupied buildings, and by a form of guerrilla theater, faced the universities with the question of what to do with students who refuse to play the game by the usual rules.

That is the main point I would like to make this evening.

Harold Taylor

The students are making the rules change by the actions they are taking. Since the universities have not been accustomed to challenges of the direct kind (whether they should be or not, I am saying they have not been accustomed to changes made by students in the rules by which they behave), there are few precedents and no traditions that can serve as models for behavior for the faculty and the administration. In the nineteenth century students rioted in order to change the colleges in which they were controlled, and pointed out to the university authorities that there was more freedom in the society outside the colleges and universities than there was in the social and political rules inside. What has developed now has been a form of instant history, in which direct action by the students, in occupying buildings, confronting deans and presidents, and seeking intransigent ways of making things happen, has produced responses of a variety of kinds by those in authority.

These range from Nathan Pusey's action in bringing in the police to the Harvard campus without consultation, without knowing what the attitudes of the university community would be to a variety of ways in which administrators have used conciliation and the law in order to put down or to cope with a new kind of intransigence. Depending on the response of the authority, the student strategy and tactics have moved from one situation to the next, until in certain situations, such as at San Francisco State, the use of police force by the authorities has produced countermeasures of force by the students, up to and including importation of bombs to the campus.

I would like to say something about Cornell, and something about San Francisco State. A great deal has been said about the guns in the hands of black students at Cornell, the threat this makes to academic freedom, to the purposes and values of American society and to the way in which education can be hamstrung. Less has been said about the black students themselves. There were 250 to 300 black students at Cornell. They were recruited from the ghettos, among other places, under the general proposition that the white universities have been too slow in providing, for public use of the black community, the facilities and the resources of university

121

life in America, and that it was time to act. Over the past three years, Cornell University recruited students from the black community—students who were brought into a white racist community at Cornell, dominated by social attitudes prevalent in the fraternity system. This system is the epitome of white racism, since it discriminates not only against blacks, but against non-Protestants and against the nonwealthy, and ends up with a social structure which is antithetical to everything that participatory democracy really means. When you bring a group of blacks into a white racist community and turn them loose, you need not wonder why, after awhile, they become hostile to the whites.

In the case of the blacks taking over Willard Straight Hall, this was a deliberate device, rhetorical theater again, to draw the attention of the total Cornell community to certain demands and requests from the black members of that community. As far as informed observers of the local situation at Cornell can tell, the reason that the blacks imported guns into the hall was that they knew that a cross was burned on the front lawn of a black dormitory the night before. Also, they had been informed that white fraternity men were coming in to take over the building, using guns. When the black students emerged on the cover of *Newsweek,* among other places, carrying guns, the entire country took this as the symbol of how far racial antagonism had gone on the country's campuses, and how the whole educational system had gotten out of hand.

We need to put this in its own perspective. After that event of the guns, the faculty of Cornell voted in its majority wisdom against allowing the students who had occupied the hall any kind of amnesty. Within twenty-four hours they reversed their decision. I suggest that this was due to the faculty's lack of comprehension of the strength of the feeling of the white students about what should be done to make a community life responsive to the needs of the blacks. It was the lack of knowledge by the faculty rather than the whimsicality of the change of votes within twenty-four hours about which we need to be worrying.

I believe that from this point on, Cornell will be a better institution now that it has had to face the reality of community attitudes, and that Cornell students' dissent has raised basic issues which were never raised before in the extremity of this condition. From now on the faculty, the administration, and the student body are going to be thinking seriously about what a university community as to be rather than what it has been.

These circumstances need to be analyzed by political scientists, by psychologists, but most of all by concerned human beings who look at the reality of the situation of the blacks and the whites, who think of education as something more than taking courses. They need to think of education as building a community in which blacks and whites, fast learners and slow learners, competitive and noncompetitive, can learn to live together.

In the case of San Francisco State, we have an example of what happens when you use force to open a college, as Governor Reagan said, with the use of "bayonets if necessary." Robert Smith, who was president of San Francisco State in November of 1968, closed down the college when confronted with the ten demands by the Black Student Union. Some were exorbitant and others reasonable. Many were already being met by plans of the faculty and the student body. There was already a Black Studies Institute, which had been developed in the student experimental college in combination with the Community Service Institute, another organization which the blacks and the whites had formed together. When the Black Student Union called a strike and presented its demands, President Smith closed the college for two days in order to hold a series of faculty, student, and administrative discussions of the whole issue. What should be done with this college at that point in American history—this was what Robert Smith was asking his college and his students to decide. As the students and faculty moved toward solutions of these problems by nonviolent means, Governor Reagan demanded that the college be opened, and Chancellor Dumke of the state colleges of California ordered Robert Smith to act accordingly. Naturally, President Smith resigned, since he knew that if he were to open the college under those circumstances he would be in for something that would amount to civil war on the campus. When Professor Hayakawa, after a telephone call from Chancellor Dumke, agreed to act as president on the understanding that he would open the college and confront the students with the police, the institution was in for three to four months of turmoil and what amounted to an internal civil war.

I believe on the evidence that had President Smith, acting on educational principle, been allowed to continue and to open the college with an agreement made, as Buell Gallagher is now opening City College in New York City, then the 134 days of turmoil, the strife, the repressive measures by the university against the students, the violence of the student militants with their bombs, their threats, and their intimidation tactics would have been avoided.

The educational point I wish to make is that the university is, should be, and must be, the center for nonviolent education, and that the answer to student dissent and student militancy must not be that of militancy and violence on the part of the university. How can students learn what it means to live in a civilized community if the answer which university and college presidents give to violence is more violence on the other side?

We are learning in this present period, as at Columbia, that the use of the regular municipal laws and authority, the appeal to court injunction is the best means of dealing with acts of violence, disruption, and militancy which go beyond the law. A student is subject to the laws of his city and country just as is the faculty, just as is the president. These laws are sufficient to take care of those actual deeds which are violent on the part of students or any other organized group. This is the way we must look at what is happening in America.

There are ways of controlling violence which are not in themselves violent. University presidents can now echo President Johnson's remark to an aide in the midst of one of his own troubled episodes: "This is the best generation of young people we have ever had, and they are all against us." In certain situations the reasons are clear. They have been stated and acted out by the young themselves. They have simply made evident, through their actions, the existence of the basic underlying sociological and political fact of Western society. The changes in post-industrial society have vastly

124

outrun the capacity of its institutions to adapt to the changes. For many students the university has become both a symbol and point of reference for the static quality of institutional bureaucracy and the sterility of the official culture. For the younger generation the university supplies the natural target for intellectual, social, and physical attack. An attack on the university is an attack on the values and structure of the society.

Daniel Cohn-Bendit's book, *Obsolete Communism: The Left Wing Alternative* (1969), in the opening pages attacks his publisher on the grounds that the publisher is trying to exploit him by paying him money to write a book. The author never resolves the question as to why he agreed to be exploited by the capitalist. In any case, Cohn-Bendit goes on to talk about the role of the student in Western society. In his conversation with Jean-Paul Sartre—who has been politically inactive for the last five years—Cohn-Bendit said this about student privileges in the life of the university:

> The defense of student interests is, in any case, very problematic. What are their so-called interests? The students don't constitute a class, the workers, the peasants, form a social class and have objective interests. Their demands are clear and are addressed to the owner hierarchy, to the representatives of the bourgeois. But the students—who are their oppressors if not the entire system of French society today?

In summary, the members of the student protest movement are speaking on behalf of those who do not express themselves so easily. The students have access to America through the mass media. They are speaking on behalf of certain moral issues, the three major ones being the war, poverty in America, and race. On those three issues the students are right. Whether or not the tactics are right by which they are trying to make their views known to the American public on the major issues, the students have raised moral and political questions for which the universities have failed to find answers.

Let me make the usual denunciation of the methods of violence used by the minority of students on the campuses. I deplore those methods of violence as much as anyone else. Students who threaten professors, or disrupt classes, or take over buildings and disrupt the entire life of the university should be subject to the regular laws against trespass and disturbing the peace. I would agree with anyone who wishes to denounce particular acts of violence by students in the contemporary university.

But I submit that on the major issues of contemporary world societies the students are right, and that the universities would not have acted on these issues had it not been for the activities and militancy of the students. This is self-evident. In the case of such a distinguished institution as Harvard University, the issues raised there included the issues of student involvement in faculty appointments, and the kind of military programs which should exist on the Harvard campus. They also questioned who should control Harvard and make the policies—should it be the Harvard corporation? By what right, ask the students, do these people in the American community outside Harvard control the entire apparatus of decision-making at Harvard? These are serious questions to which Harvard has now begun to address itself. It is certain that without those eight thousand students in the football stadium, voting on whether or not to have a strike against a university which they love, these issues would not have been raised.

Now, we must take seriously things we have not been taking seriously until students raised the issues before our eyes. What responsibility does the university, as a corporate institution, have to military research, to the progress of a war in which the young people are involved to their own peril, and in which older people have decided they should become involved? In what way should the system of education be reformed, so that the students have a direct part in making decisions about policy having to do with social, political, and intellectual issues on the campuses? In what way can we now make a community out of what has been a fragmented set of people, trustees, administration, faculty, students, alumni? How can we make a community out of this conglomerate set of fragmented and sometimes hostile groups?

What should be the content of the contemporary curriculum

126

for undergraduates? Should the undergraduate college be simply a breeding place to produce people for the graduate schools, to produce people to feed the manpower needs of American society? These are serious and important questions which have been raised by militant students, but which are also being raised by those who are not as militant. James Kunen, in his own judgment, was radicalized by what happened at Columbia. But as one reads his book, one finds in his nineteen-year-old vocabulary, in his attitude toward himself, in his comments on education, his parents, America, and the world, a spirit of critical, compassionate liberalism, which in certain circumstances becomes revolutionary. Revolutionary, that is, in the true sense, which is to say that young men of his kind want to change society. In order to change the society, they want to change its educational system.

When the matter is put this way, you find you are talking about at least 95 per cent of the students in the protest movement. We must pay more attention to what Calvin Plimpton of Amherst College said in his letter to President Nixon—that problems exist in America, the problems of war and the attitude to war taken by the Administration, the attitude to poverty, the attitude to race —and that until these problems are tackled head-on, vigorously, with an amount of idealism at least equivalent to that which the younger generation is showing, we will not have a cessation of campus dissent. These are the social, political, and moral problems which the universities must tackle. Until they do, the younger generation is going to keep pressing them upon us.

What we now must do, then, is to look seriously at the quality of life within our campus communities. We must arrange a new kind of community in which the students can be dealt with seriously as equal citizens in a community of learning. The faculty have a role to play in teaching, the students have a role to play in learning, and the administration has a role to play in helping the teachers teach and the students learn. The students need to learn more than how to master academic subjects; they need to learn how to live. In order to learn how to live, they need to be taught how to live by the principled example of those in the faculty and administration who are in possession of intelligence, in possession of the facts, and who can speak to the young with authenticity. The young now judge the older generation by the standards they apply to themselves, as athletes and musicians judge each other by how well they play, not by how well they talk. The younger generation lacks piety toward authority and toward the older generation. We must look to the older generation to test its own authenticity against the judgments of the young. Then we can begin to see whether or not we, in the universities, can respond to the young in authentic terms and justify what we believe and what we do against not merely youth's criticism of ourselves, but against the eternal questions that intelligent, wise, and tough-minded people always raise. It is now necessary to give expression to our own views, to allow the young to test us in terms of our willingness to change the society, to change our educational institutions, and to change them in ways more consonant with the wisdom of the young.

PART THREE

INSTITUTIONAL
RESPONSE

James A. McCain

Unrest on
the Campus

9

With crisis succeeding crisis on today's campus, only the foolhardy
would venture a final pronouncement on the scope of our student
disorders and what to do about them. Nevertheless, some facts and
implications are clearly discernible, even as turmoil mounts, and
here I wish to examine them. The bare facts of the case are
shocking: unruly mobs of university students, some of them
armed, have been disrupting classes, barricading themselves in
buildings, assaulting teachers and administrators, confiscating and

publishing confidential files, and destroying millions of dollars' worth of property. More than one university has been closed down completely.

The general public has been outraged by this behavior. Because of the university's unique reliance on public understanding and support in order to survive as a haven of free intellectual inquiry, the effect of this behavior on the public is a matter of great concern. The facts about campus unrest are matters of general information, but the public, nevertheless, is misinformed. Because public mistrust of universities and their administrators is intensified by this misinformation, every reasonable effort should be made to set the record straight, through contacts with alumni and parents and effective use of the communications media, to which all universities have access. The public should be reminded, for example, that by no means have all our colleges and universities been racked by disorders. In actual fact, less than 10 per cent have suffered such afflictions, although these include some of the most prestigious such as Harvard, Columbia, and California.

Nor are student protest and violence a new phenomenon. The rioting by University of Paris students last summer pales in comparison with the pitched battles fought by students in that same university eight centuries ago when hundreds of lives were lost. Today's draft card burner is a spiritual descendant of students of the 1930s in this country who signed the Oxford oath pledging never to bear arms in defense of their country.

People generally are confused about the nature of the students involved. It cannot be stressed too often that the extremists are a tiny minority representing less than 2 per cent of total university populations. An interesting facet of this subject was noted by John Fischer (1968) in *Harper's* when he pointed out that today's student extremists are almost entirely majors in theoretical disciplines, principally the humanities, the arts, and social sciences, whereas those studying in the professional fields, students with a "life purpose," to use his phrase, are never found on the barricades. The large majority of today's undergraduates are quite possibly the most responsible and idealistic students ever to attend our universities, a fact certainly obscured by the militant few. In fact, we must grudgingly admit that even the troublemakers are, by and large, youth of superior intelligence activated by idealism, regardless of how grossly it is misdirected.

I fear the public has gained the impression that, because of cowardice, indecision, or poor judgment, college administrators generally have been unwilling to employ forthright measures to prevent disorders or to end them once they start, and take appropriate disciplinary action after the fact. It is generally assumed, for example, that presidents and deans possess absolute authority under which they can summarily dismiss student offenders. In actual fact, the courts have held, albeit recently, that the principles of due process must be followed in the administration of student discipline.

More important, although some institutions have admittedly been slack or even irresponsible in coping with destructive students, the great majority have responded with severe disciplinary action. For example, two recent issues of American Council on Education bulletins have cited recent disciplinary action, in many cases permanent expulsion, affecting well over a thousand students in a score of universities.

Despite general disapproval of student militants, many laymen assume these militants must reflect serious deficiencies in American higher education. Shortcomings exist. (However, in many of their programs, our universities are better than ever, specifically in their professional curriculums and in mathematics and the sciences.) Perhaps the most fundamental question has to do with the extent to which universities have been insensitive to their own deficiencies or reluctant to undertake desirable improvements. Today's students are far more sensitive than their predecessors to shortcomings in their educational experiences, whether these be uninspiring teachers, excessive use of graduate teaching assistants, the emphasis on research at the expense of education, the perfunctory nature of many advisory services, the impersonal atmosphere of the multiversity, or the lack of relevance in portions of the curriculum.

This final issue makes an excellent case in point. Many of you will recall the general education movement which originated more than thirty years ago and was clearly articulated by the Harvard faculty in the volume, *General Education in a Free Society* (Harvard Committee, 1945). The term *relevance* was a key to this movement, as it is in much of today's student protest—how to relate the content of instruction, especially in the humanities and social sciences, to the realities of the world about us.

I recall one horrible example from this earlier period. It was the student who complained that his class in Marriage and the Family never got beyond the eighteenth century. Yet despite three decades of effort, only minimal changes have been made in the liberal arts curriculum. We are doing business in the same old way. It may be that parliaments do not reform themselves; universities can and must.

We have been singularly unsuccessful in mobilizing the opinions of the responsible majority of students as an effective countermeasure to the extremist few. I can offer no ready-made formula for achieving this strategy, but certain propositions are worthy of consideration.

Interference with classes, the blockading of buildings, and destruction of property must be clearly revealed to the campus community for what they are: infringement on the rights and freedom of others. Those in positions of authority must make known their concern for the majority thus affronted. When extremists successfully employ force to gain their ends and intolerable behavior goes unpunished, the rank and file of responsible students become understandably cynical about the rewards of virtue. Such feelings are no doubt compounded when disproportionate numbers of the extremist element are invited into the highest councils of university government. When university officials involve students, as they should, in planning programs and in decision-making at all levels, it is critically important that those thus employed be representative of the entire student population.

In fact, the strategy of coping with campus disorders has,

to date, left much to be desired. For at least three years, danger signals should have been apparent well in advance of the advent of violence on many campuses. Yet surprisingly few officials had planned and announced what their response would be. Equivocation over the use of outside law enforcement agencies has given heart to those bent on destruction. Abhorrent as the employment of state troopers or local policemen is to university tradition, it goes without saying that the alternative to such a policy is much worse when extremists not only endanger life and property, but place in jeopardy the present and future intellectual integrity of higher education. Certainly one of the most distressing tactics employed at some institutions has been to buy off the offenders by meeting their demands on the spot. Anyone even slightly familiar with Pavlov's experiments will recognize this as an invitation to further violence when goals are difficult to achieve. Regardless of how meritorious the demands, university authorities should not accede to them at the point of a gun.

Finally, universities have yet to determine how students can contribute most effectively to their governance. It is enormously to their credit that this is our first generation of students actively concerned over the quality of their education and determined to contribute to its improvement. Many of us have long since discovered that students can be trusted to behave responsibly and worthily when assigned authority in all important areas of student life and activity. Today, happily, our colleges and universities are developing measures for involving students in the evaluation of teaching, in the development of the curriculum, in the improvement of academic regulation, and, for that matter, in policy formation at the highest levels of administration.

However, the limitations on the student's capacity to contribute must be recognized, hopefully by the student himself. The transient nature of the student population is a case in point. The student leader's brief exposure to the campus often limits his capacity for wise and informed decision-making in some areas. Furthermore, the turnover in student leadership poses difficulties for continuity of policy. More important, the student whose education is incomplete is handicapped in passing judgment on the educational process. Nevertheless, we should exploit fully this unprecedented student interest in the effectiveness of the educational program by assigning students an appropriate role in those councils of the university responsible for the evaluation and improvement of programs.

A situation as fluid as the one here under discussion defies summary. Nevertheless, agreement might be found to a few conclusions.

Student disorders confront American higher education with a crisis the possible consequences of which are unthinkable. Our measures, to date, for coping with these disorders have been less than effective. In fact, a new dimension is being added to the problem as vigilante tactics by conservative students threaten the campus with civil war. At stake are two assets indispensable to the survival of our colleges and universities: public confidence and support, and freedom to manage our own affairs. It is essential that each college and university adopt procedures to prevent destruction and disruption on its own campus. It is desirable that the nation's colleges and universities collaborate in efforts to develop a national policy for meeting this crisis.

I cannot emphasize too strongly the fact that we are all in this together. The policy at one institution, if it is the wrong policy, hurts us all. If it is the right policy, it reinforces what we should do. Quite obviously, then, American higher education is in peril today as never before—and the outcome is by no means settled. When the bell tolls at Cornell or at Harvard, as John Donne pointed out centuries ago, it tolls for all of us.

Commentary

Nancy S. Cole

Only a short time ago I was a student, so this may be the reason that I will attempt to emphasize the good students and not the bad ones. In between my anger and frustrations over student violence I have been forced to admit the students' often candid perception of the world. First to regard the tiny minority of violent rock-throwing, gun-toting, building-occupying, revolutionary students as "the problem of student unrest" is to ignore the probably greater problem of the thinking, questioning, dissatisfied large portion of students. For it is not the militants who are closing down our college campuses, but to a large measure the moderate students with considerable sympathy and support for the militants. While we can likely agree about our dislike of violence, there is much less agreement about how to deal with this larger student unrest. We express belief in a free university governed by reason, but thoughtful students are often raising the issue, "Why must we reason within such a confining framework that the results of our reasoning are not reasonable?" Their questions are: "Is the university really ruled by reason?" "Is the United States Government really ruled by reason?" "Is it reasonable that the richest country in the history of the world must have poverty?" "Is it reasonable that the powerful nations must race each other in building potentially world-destroying weapons?" "Is racial prejudice in ghettos reasonable?" "Is it reasonable that a university should underpay its cafeteria workers and janitors while supporting in high style essentially professional athletics?" Now, do not be too quick to answer, "No, it's not reasonable, but be realistic." I submit that at its best the student unrest in this country is begging us to answer instead, "No, it's not reasonable and there must be a better way to deal with the question than to accept unreason."

137

Issues of the Seventies

Robert L. Ewigleben

Everything that happens to a university or college town, or near the campus, today, is a college problem. We have a job to do to straighten the media people out on some of these things. That campus unrest is a big business is evident in the media today. We have a job to do with the media to include positive ideas and keep straightening them out. It will be a long time before we build any buildings in the state of California because the public has spoken and is saying to us, "Get your house in order." It is high time that we do get our house in order. By that, I do not mean come up with necessarily repressive measures; I mean manage our institutions, involve our students in decision-making, and move ahead, making the best use of this opportunity for change that is with us. I really question whether our universities are better than ever. Certainly our young people are saying they are not. I still see the lecturer up in front, quite often before hundreds of people. I still do not see instructional technology being utilized. And I have never seen colleges, even the land-grant universities, relating themselves to the community as our students are demanding that we relate ourselves to the community. We have missed this altogether, and I do not see these efforts in the magnitude that they should exist. Demands that are meritorious should be met before they are ever presented. That does not mean that you say yes to everything. But, certainly, we had many things pointed out to us where we were grossly deficient. We should have known about those things before the students had to bring them to us and point them out in ways in which they did. Our black students many times hold meetings. They just put up "TCB" and that means Take Care of Business. I think that all of us should put up our signs and start really taking care of business.

Ronald B. Thompson

A little over a year ago our administration building was taken over by some thirty-four black students. I tried to reach my

138

wife to tell her what was going on. I could not reach her. As she came in the door the telephone rang. She answered, and they said, "Is your husband there?" She said, "Why, no, he's at the university." They said, "This telephone call is to tell you that he'll never get home," and they hung up. Any person or group of persons asking the right to make the decisions must be in a position to assume responsibility for that position and that decision. This I think is fundamental. We still live in an age of responsibility. To me, we must control the situation to the point where we can carry on a discussion. Whether we meet force with force we will not have gained much if the university is completely destroyed. I have another conviction that the people who are asking to make decisions must be in a position to offer a positive constructive program. Thus far too many students come to us organized only to destroy and not to build. On the assumption that what we have is wrong they will destroy everything we have, by revolution, rather than improve it by evolution. It seems to me that our only hope is to converse, to carry on conversation, communication and solve these problems.

Daniel D. Robinson

Who's Managing?

10

There is a great deal of interest these days in improving college and university management; witness the rash of meetings and discussions on long-range planning, management information systems, planning models, and the like—topics which, only a few short years ago, were seldom referred to in college management circles. We can better understand these new tools if we reflect a bit on how the interest in them has grown to its present proportions.

We are all aware of the tremendous growth in higher education since World War II. Mostly we think of increased enrollments and maybe increased costs. If we look more carefully, we will also see much greater complexity all the way from program offerings to payroll procedures. Costs have been rising faster in higher education than in the economy at large. The pressures to provide new faculty, supporting staff, and facilities have grown faster than enrollment. Research activity and involvement in providing non-instructional services to the community have increased in scope, depth, and competition with instruction for faculty, facilities, and finances. The importance of state-financed colleges and universities has increased faster than higher education as a whole, reflecting the continuing shift in enrollments from private to public institutions. The federal government has become more active and influential in shaping the patterns of college and university behavior, adding increased demands with each new program.

All of this has happened at a time when some of the most fundamental academic programs of colleges and universities are being looked at simultaneously as both irrelevant and the only salvation for the ills of society. Student unrest, while disturbing in itself, mirrors a deep-seated sense of uneasiness about society's value system on a larger basis. Technology continues to move ahead at a faster rate each year, widening the chasm between it and the society it is intended to serve. Thus the bridge which education is supposed to provide grows longer, harder to build, and more precarious by the year.

For these reasons and many more, a growing number of people in higher education have come to believe that we cannot simply go on doing things as they have been done before. We are in a period which on the one hand provides more resources than ever before and on the other indicates that there are limits on how much can be made available. Higher education must cope with the discipline of constrained choice. No college or university, private or public, now has or can hope to have the resources needed to do everything well. An institution will have to decide whether to do a few things well or many things poorly. There is no alternative.

Higher education has passed the point where an adminis-

141

trator can smile benignly at each new crisis, secure in the thought that, no matter what, everything always turns out all right in the end. We already have clear evidence of institutions which have had to pay a very high price for shortsighted administration. A number of others are fast approaching that same crisis. As demands on resources from other sectors of our society continue to grow, the pressure on higher education will become enormous. Efforts to make better use of what resources are available are imperative if we are to survive.

The role of administration in this crisis has become much more important than it has ever been in the past. This change is really a change in perception, since good management has always been beneficial to colleges; the difference today is that it is becoming easier to recognize the symptoms of bad management, and that the realization that good management is important in an institution of higher learning is growing. Until recently most academic administrators believed (or certainly behaved as if they believed) that colleges were not subject to the same kinds of management rules as other organizations; that through some sort of marvelous beneficence, they were exempt from all or most of the consequences of bad management. This revelation, this insight, this slow coming of age has finally made possible the rational consideration of the need to fashion tools that will assist in meeting the management problems of colleges and universities.

All of the management techniques which are new to higher education are not themselves new. They were first developed to meet management problems in industry or government. It is their application to higher education which is new. Innovation here, then, is accomplished by finding new uses for old tools. To do this effectively, differences as well as similarities must be considered. While colleges need to be businesslike, they are not businesses. Education cannot be directly equated with underkill and overkill. The motivations of educators are somewhat different from those of soap manufacturers. Or if they are not inherently different, they have become so because of the differences in the reward systems each enterprise has developed over many years.

Daniel D. Robinson

While the needs are varied and touch every aspect of activity, there are four main areas where improved tools for college management are sorely needed, namely, organizational structure; planning, budgeting, and operating control; operating systems; and management information systems. These areas are interrelated, but each should be considered separately so that the needs and the tools to meet those needs may be more easily perceived.

Many college presidents have nurtured an abhorrence of organizational charts. No wonder then that if you want to know who is managing, you cannot find out. Either everyone is or no one is. It is not just the president's fault, although he is in the best position to correct the problem. Most academic people are frightened by organizational charts. Many creative professional people in other types of enterprises have a similar reaction. After all, who wants to be put in a box?

The chart, of course, is not what we are interested in since it usually is not explicit enough to be useful. The important concepts are the identification of what an individual is responsible for and his concurrent authority, and how each person or function relates to the other in the total organization. No college president, dean, or business manager achieves very much by himself. Yet each has duties to perform which the others do not. It is a synergistic relationship which is sought, not one which inhibits initiative and creativity.

The historical development and unique functions of higher education introduce special problems to its organization. Faculty and students have long established policies and controlled various activities central to the life of the college. These activities often place significant long-term demands on the limited resources available to the institution. The participation of faculty and students in the management process, therefore, must be conducted so that irresponsibility, parochialism, and myopia are not encouraged.

In trying to cope with these problems, a number of colleges have attempted to define more clearly their organizational structure. Particular interest seems to be centering on the role of the department chairman, or in the small college, the division head. The

143

department chairman has the most immediate contact with the faculty. Often he teaches, too, and thus maintains contact with students in the classroom. His role has been perceived differently by each of the constituents of the college community, including himself. Yet now there is a growing awareness of the essential role he can play in the whole college management process.

Seldom have department chairmen been selected for their proven proficiency in management. Even less frequently have they been rewarded for performing such duties well. Similarly, seldom are department chairmen removed from their posts when they do not manage well. These conditions do not encourage the development of department chairmen as effective managers. On the other hand, if an institution expects to have department chairmen perform the functions of first-line management, some changes will have to be made. Their new responsibilities, authority, and relationship to others will have to be clearly defined. They will have to be given the training and support required to perform these new tasks. Judgment and appropriate acknowledgment of their performance in this new role are also imperative.

Even while this new role of department chairman is being developed by some, there are others who are convinced that another answer is needed. Many educators are struggling to find ways to introduce innovation into the curriculum faster and more effectively than in the past. The academic department, with its relatively narrow discipline concerns, has been the bulwark against change in many instances. New approaches to curriculum development give emphasis to interdisciplinary programs, which call for the creation of new hybrid departments or for borrowing faculty from the usual departmental structure. Both techniques have serious drawbacks. In either case the role of the department chairman is critical.

While there never will be any final or absolute detailed solution to the problems of organizational structure, certain principles can be extracted from the preceding discussion, namely, that the need to define authority, responsibility, and interrelationships will always be present—failure to do so always will be costly; and

144

that organizational structure should be designed to facilitate organizational goals—when they conflict, the institution will be ineffective.

Once we acknowledge that organizational structure and institutional goals must be congruent, we admit to the need for institutional goals. This implies that planning of some sort is taking place in the college. Until fairly recently, this would be a hopelessly naive assumption. In relatively recent years, some colleges have been encouraged to prepare so-called long-range plans. Typically these have been projections of one sort or another for a ten-year period. Some of these institutions went even further by attempting to live for a number of years within the confines of such a plan. It has been popular for many years to have an architect develop a "master campus plan," sometimes referred to simply as the "master plan." Such plans too often were unconcerned with the academic goals of the college. More than likely, if the college had any explicit academic goals, few people knew what they were.

Fortunately, there is a growing awareness that much of the planning that has been done before has been largely ineffective. Certain characteristics of good planning have emerged from the experience of others. These can be of benefit to college administrators if properly adapted to their needs.

First of all, planning should be concerned primarily with academic goals. College faculty and administrators often revel in their uniqueness, the pluralism of higher education, and the like. Immediately thereafter, they attempt to emulate all of the programs of every other institution. Clearly this is not possible, and probably is not even desirable. Choices must be made. The choices must be feasible. They ought to be relevant to the needs of some segment of society. If planning does not focus on academic goals, the vacuum will be filled by some less meaningful consideration and here, parenthetically, I may add that it will probably be done by the business manager.

Second, institutional goals ultimately have to be described in sufficient detail so that they can be quantified. Only then can decisions be converted into action. College governing boards, faculty, and administrators have always been involved in considerations of quality, role, mission, character, and other unquantified attributes of their institutions. Some say that the act of quantification itself will destroy the essence of the underlying concept of quality. Others will point out that there are too many unknowns in the whole academic process to be able to quantify with any degree of assurance. Granted these truths, actions are ultimately taken in quantified form respecting programs, students, faculty, space, and money. Some way ought to exist of at least attempting to relate these actions to what the college is trying to achieve.

Third, some attempt must be made to assess the long-range impact of proposed programs on institutional resources, namely, faculty and staff, facilities, and money. Two important concepts are subsets of this principle. The first of these is that to embark on a program which cannot be supported is foolhardy and dangerous. The second is that there are usually a variety of alternative specific programs which will satisfy a given set of academic goals. Each should be examined and the best feasible plan selected.

The examination of alternatives is a complex procedure. It involves many intricate relationships and a great deal of computation and analysis. Some colleges are designing mathematical models which will simulate the demands on resources over a period of years of alternative mixes and levels of program activity. By programming such a model on a computer, a great variety of alternatives can be calculated quickly. The decisions respecting programs to be selected would still be controlled by people, not by the machine.

The last characteristic of good long-range planning which colleges need to recognize is that it is a continuing, dynamic activity rather than a static one. No individual or group can anticipate the future with accuracy or certainty. The environment changes. New needs emerge and old programs become irrelevant. Sources of support change, presenting new opportunities and eliminating some of the old ones. Thus the planning process has to provide for the continuous examination of goals, programs, and alternatives.

Budgeting might be contrasted with planning in terms of time span, detail, and degree of commitment. An operating budget usually relates to one year while a long-range plan treats with at least five or more years. The budget contains much more detail than the long-range plan. Finally, the budget, once approved, usually represents an absolute commitment of resources while the long-range plan will be reviewed and changed many times before actual implementation.

Budgeting is a process which has been practiced by many colleges for years. Most institutions, in fact, will have a budget, even though they do not have an organizational chart. The problem is that the budget philosophy and technique most often used have been ineffectual. Most colleges have used an incremental approach to preparing and approving each new year's budget. Whatever has been approved in the latest current budget is used as a base for the following year. From that point on, only changes from that base are scrutinized or even discussed. Budget documentation is usually limited to a display of the resources required. Seldom are these requirements related to the output of the activity being financed. Similarly, the output of the activity is seldom related to the long-range goals of the institution.

The recent emphasis on long-range planning has led some to believe that no real improvement can be made in the annual budgeting process until a long-range plan has been developed. This is not true for an institution which is already in operation. In fact, it may be helpful for some to defer long-range planning efforts until basic improvements are made in the annual budgeting process. Two steps that can be taken to improve budgeting are, first, start the process earlier. Most colleges do not begin early enough, thus forcing fundamental issues to be cast aside in haste. Revisions can always be made as the actual year approaches. Second, have each department build its budget needs based on what it intends to do, what services it expects to perform. Program output should be described in sufficient detail to support requirements for people, space, equipment, and money.

Once the flow of budget data provides both cost and output information, the question "why" can be asked. The objective is to break away from the incremental budget concept. After that

147

philosophy is discarded, it will become increasingly apparent that the "why" question is not answered satisfactorily since there is no agreed-upon frame of reference for the reply. This then leads naturally into the evolution of long-range plans based upon academic objectives.

The annual operating budget may have a long history in college management, but it has not been used as a control device in a constructive manner in all cases. Many colleges prepare and approve budgets and never try to use them as guides in operation or as a basis for evaluating performance. In some cases, the financial and statistical reports of actual results are not categorized in the same way as the budget. Some colleges do not give copies of the approved budget to those who are supposed to spend the money. Later they wonder why there are problems.

There has been much confusion in colleges about budget control responsibilities. Typically the controller or business manager is held responsible for overdrafts, while everyone else is given a blank check to commit institutional funds. This gets back to the question of organizational control and responsibility and the disparity between authority and responsibility. The result usually is the development of elaborate, costly, time-consuming procedures used by the business manager to protect himself from censure. Everyone else spends all of his time trying to beat the system.

Many people are involved in the operation of a college. Thus each is responsible for the activity under his control. He should be held responsible for what he does both as to the output of his department and the resources he uses. If this management philosophy is followed, the budget becomes a useful operating tool. The control mechanisms built into the operating systems can be kept simple and yet will be more effective.

There are in any college many organized activities and procedures which can be classified as operating systems. Admissions, registration, classroom scheduling, payroll, library cataloging, cash receipts, cash disbursements, purchasing, and the like are examples. Basically they serve as the means of getting done something which is necessary to the college's existence. While each has its own objectives, most are related to one or more of the others.

Probably most of the improvement to date in college management has been in the area of operating systems. A great deal has been done to make individual systems more efficient and effective. Less frequently the interdependence of various operating systems has been taken into consideration when designing systems changes. Once again, the influence of good organization is felt. Dealing effectively with improvement of operating systems often requires close cooperation among two or more departments of a college. If all see these improvements as shared responsibilities, the results will generally be better.

Many colleges have been able to borrow ideas, if not entire systems, from other colleges which appear to have solved their operating problems satisfactorily. Some operating systems are particularly sensitive to differences in institutional policies, organization structure, and other characteristics which might be unique. Care should be exercised, therefore, when either borrowing from others or developing one's own systems, to see that these peculiarities are accommodated or changed.

Management information systems can be thought of as the link between the planning-budgeting-operating-control functions of management and the operating systems through which activities are accomplished. One of the more recent phenomena in the evolution of college management is the realization that information can be useful in the decision-making process. The major objective of a management information system, therefore, is to provide useful, relevant information to management in the form and at the time when it would be most useful.

All operating systems generate data. Most use data in order to function. Many activities, systems and decisions need the same data at different times. The management information system should provide for the capture, classification, storage, and retrieval of data in a manner which will facilitate the entire management function.

Because of the volume of information involved and the complexity of the interrelationships, most people automatically associate a management information system with a computer. Logically, if an institution can use a large-scale system effectively, the investment in system design, programming, and operation will be worthwhile. In the long run, the large universities probably will find operation without such a system impractical. This may not be true, however, for the small college.

Management information system design involves a consideration of all of the areas discussed earlier as well as others. It is imperative that the overall design of the system and the interrelationship of its parts be thoroughly planned before starting on any part of it, particularly if this involves commitment to a specific computer configuration. A great deal of money, time, and effort have been wasted because of the failure to invest a relatively modest sum in preliminary planning. This early planning stage is useful, even in itself, because of the searching inquiry it requires.

The small college had better give an effort of this sort extensive consideration before becoming committed. Much can be done to improve the flow of information in a small college without getting involved in complex computer operations. The first obstacle usually present in a small college which can be approached without cost concerns the feelings of people about their proprietary rights to data. Not infrequently the chief accountant and the registrar have useful information in their files. The trouble is that the information does not reach anyone else in the college. Another problem is that the correct interrelationships in data classification are not built into the data classifications currently being used. If the systems are mostly manual, changes of this sort can be made very easily. Changes can be made in a simple way in a small college which can improve substantially the usefulness of the information they are already collecting.

In the end analysis, these new techniques cannot in themselves provide the answers to all of the problems currently facing higher education. In order that a college accomplish its purposes, people must be willing to define and establish what those purposes are. The cry for change in every aspect of our society is loud on all fronts. Nowhere has it been louder or more noticeable than in higher education. Sometimes change can occur only in the face of crisis. If that is so, then higher education not only has available the tools better to manage its affairs and encourage innovation; it has the motivation as well.

Commentary

John J. Coffelt

Much of the trouble institutions are now having stems from the fact that people simply cannot find who has the responsibility for making management decisions. Too much management flexibility can cause great confusion and misunderstanding when people try to find out who is really running the shop. Because policies have not been clear, people at second and third levels of management have had to make operational decisions. Registrars and directors of admission in some cases have not themselves been able to find out what the institution's policies are, and so they have had to make on-the-spot decisions. This worked fine until their decisions were challenged. But now they are being questioned; students are asking, "Who says so? What is the rule? Where is it written down?" This challenge of authority becomes an even greater problem as we broaden the base of participation, as various interest groups get involved in the policy-making process. You find that as you move toward group involvement it becomes a very agonizing process on the campus, that policy formulation comes to be much more a political exercise than an intellectual activity.

Oluf M. Davidsen

All too often, it seems that long-range planning in higher education is focused on the structure rather than the functions of the institution. Most planning activities revolve around departments, facilities, personnel, and equipment. These are the *means* of education. Because of their visibility and reality, they often seem to substitute for *goals* in educational planning. Rarely is educational planning based on questions such as: What do we wish to achieve? What will this or that facility or position contribute toward that goal? If provided, how can its contribution to the goal be assessed?

In the end, educational planning must be based on some criteria against which to measure educational effectiveness. Traditionally, these criteria or goals are stated in lofty language and are correspondingly difficult to measure. They do not have to be. Almost every institution—whatever its official goals—can obtain a measure of its effectiveness by seeking answers to questions such as: How many students enroll who do not finish? What characterizes the students who do not finish? As against those who do? Are these characteristics discernible at the time the students first enroll? What implications do these findings have for planning with respect to facilities, programs, equipment?

Phillip G. Hubbard

There is a strong force tending to tear the institution apart and it is necessary to give continual attention to the management in order to hold it together. I would like first to refer to the effects that sources of financial support have upon the management. A drastic increase in tuition is only the first step in a continuing assault upon the base of support, deliberately shifted to students. This coincides with the drive by both faculty and students to become more heavily involved with the management of the university. They insist that they should have a very strong voice. The people to whom that support is being shifted feel that they deserve

152

a greater voice in the operation. The committee system which has grown up in most institutions is an inevitable consequence. The people who are responsible for making decisions must contact all of the people who wish to influence those decisions and yet do it in such a way that authority is commensurate with the responsibilities.

Robert Heinich

Technology and the Student

11

We will have to use technology on a more massive scale than ever before in order to help the student. I know many readers will say that the student resents technology; he resents our attempts to mechanize him and the campus. But the fact of the matter is that he does not resent technology. What he resents is use of technology for our purposes rather than for his.

The IBM card is virtually a universal symbol of mechanization on the campus, but students use other computerized services without qualms, including dating by computer, although I hate to see a machine come between boy meets girl. But adjustments are made. In a cartoon I saw recently, a young man was saying to an attractive girl sitting behind a desk, "Miss Smith, I'm Roger Davis from personnel and I had to see if you were everything your IBM card said you were." Widening the base of information handling broadens the selection process.

Seriously, rather than resenting technology, students are expert at assimilating and using it. We always underestimate the amount of technology the young absorb, and their skill at manipulating what they do absorb, partly because we tend to project into them the uncertainties we feel toward new technological developments.

Students not only must learn more today, but they also must be able to manage more sophisticated information handling techniques than any previous generation. This starts at an early age with complex toys manipulated expertly, with intuitive rather than explicit understanding—that may come much later. Because toys reflect the technology of the moment, children who grow up without benefit of mastering them may be severely handicapped as students, and then as adults. But the toys I am talking about are expensive, which means the very people who cannot afford to be without these experiences cannot buy them.

Of course, the poor get hold of as much as they can. Three years ago, my wife and I were in the home of a poor Mexican family in Los Angeles. In the middle of the conversation, their eight-year-old daughter burst into the house carrying one half of a walkie-talkie set. In heavily accented English, she was saying, "Tony, do you read me? Tony, do you read me?" She and her friends were exploring the capabilities of an information handling system that from then on, to them, would take its place in the natural order of things. I was struck also by the conscious precision of language. The accent was pronounced, but she had a great respect for the specific vocabulary associated with this form of communication. However, the disadvantaged do not get enough of this level of experience and federal programs like Head Start should make sure this important step in information handling is solidly built in.

That today's college students welcome, understand, and use technology when their own ends are to be served comes through very clearly in the recent and current waves of student protests. When the protests started, the universities seemed to believe they were still intellectual islands in the best European tradition, while the students were living in McLuhan's total environment. Communication was instantaneous and network television was intuitively used as a prime means of spreading information and tactics. And, of course, television was used as a tactic. The students took the middle-class money they resented to buy air transportation (technology) to Chicago and other cities, where they gathered frequently at New Left conventions to hammer out policy (or nonpolicy), exchange tactics, and conduct school. The lessons taught at these sessions are quite detailed. For an interesting example, I refer you to Joseph Schwab's recent book (1969), *College Curriculum and Student Protest,* in which he reports the techniques of speech and posture taught as the best with which to intimidate a student-faculty meeting. But the point is that technology is so taken for granted in this context, so ingrained in the bone, that the students do not even stop to think that they could not mount their protests without it. In microcosm it is like the teenage folksinger attacking technology, accompanying himself on an electric guitar.

By the way, professors were on those planes, too—on their way to RAND, the Pentagon, GM, and so forth.

But the attachment the young have for technology comes through most strongly and obviously in entertainment. The favored means of expression of youth today are all technologically oriented. (In one case, I hasten to add, technology only facilitates—in the form of a pill.) When we speak of students resenting technology, we should pause to consider film, TV, light shows, mixed-media displays, incredibly (and harmfully) amplified music, and so on. A high point of some sort was reached last year when the debut of the new Symphony of New York featured a multi-media interpretation of Berlioz' *Symphonie Fantastique,* to the delight of hippies, dowagers and other members of the establishment, and two hundred kids from Harlem.

The young do not reject technology. They do reject mechanization. Phillip Jackson (1968), in the slender volume *The Teacher and the Machine,* discusses human mechanization and defines it as "the process by which people are treated mechanically; that is, without giving thought to what is going on inside them" (pp. 75–85). His specific illustration of human mechanization is devoid of technology; it shows, rather, how attention, assignments, learning tasks, and discussion can be mechanized by the human voice. He lists six ways in which students may be mechanized, or treated mechanically: We turn them on and off whenever it suits our fancy. It is unnecessary to offer an explanation of why they are working. They are owned (no plans and future of their own; or unwillingly they relinquish their own plans and energies). They are all work; idleness is waste. A machine or a human's worth is judged by the quality of its products. There is an absence of human empathy (no need to feel sorry for a machine that functions improperly).

It may be readily seen from this list that people do not need machines to treat other people mechanically. On the other hand, as Paul Goodman (1969) has pointed out, and this may surprise some of you, when each student is treated as an individual, instructional technology becomes not only acceptable, but also most meaningful to him. If he is not recognized as an individual, technology then makes the school experience still more rigid and impersonal. But it is clearly our perception of the student and how we treat him which determines whether we humanize or dehumanize him. If we perceive him properly, technology can help us do the instructional job much more effectively.

Not long ago, Daniel Bell, in his report to Columbia College (1966), made this recommendation (while pertaining to English, the essential problems are present in many other junior division courses):

> The course in freshman English today is taught by thirty different members of the English department. A course like

English is extremely costly to the college, especially at a time when salaries are rising sharply and teaching schedules are being reduced. Given the general upgrading that is taking place in the secondary schools, it is entirely the responsibility of these schools to assure the proficiency of their students in English composition. . . . Under certain conditions, a student might be admitted to college with composition as a deficiency. But it would then be *his* obligation, not the college's, to make up this deficiency, either by studying composition in the summertime, at extra cost, or in some form of tutoring outside the college schedule [p. 239].

One might quibble with Bell about his assumption of homogeneity and its desirability, but his observation in terms of what was happening in the secondary schools to then college-bound youth was sound.

Two-and-a-half years later his crystal ball has become densely clouded. His own university is committed to a policy, most of which is voluntary and part of which is forced, which will pull his basic assumption right out from under him. Universities and colleges throughout the country have stepped up recruitment programs in ghetto areas which will result in extremely heterogeneous freshman classes.

My own university is vigorously pursuing such a program under the leadership of an assistant dean who is, fortunately, black. This summer an intensive remedial program, principally in English, and headed by a black, will help give these students a fighting chance in September. However, the cost will *not* be picked up by the students, but by the university and private individuals. Meanwhile, other universities and colleges are simply opening their doors. Rutgers has announced that branches in certain attendance centers will take any who apply. The freshman class this September, and in subsequent Septembers, will reflect a great range in achievement, as we measure it.

It seems to me that, in this situation, heavy reliance must be placed on technologies of instruction which can account for large variations in student achievement. Normal or large-group instruction techniques may be used with the large portion of the freshman class entering at the achievement level that Bell expected. For those substantially below this level, individually prescribed instruction (IPI)' programs, heavily supported by tutorial techniques when appropriate, will be able to correct deficiencies most effectively. The IPI programs I have in mind would be patterned substantially after the ones in Pittsburgh, Duluth, and certain other public school systems. Behaviorally based instruction, with strong influence from identification psychology in preparation of materials, will give these students the security they badly need as they acquire the knowledge and skills required to make them competitive.

This would be an excellent opportunity to experiment with Computer Administered Instruction (CAI)' in remedial programs. Since many of the learning problems of these students will be similar, networks of terminals on many campuses linked to a central computer may be established, bringing down the per-pupil costs of what is normally pretty expensive instruction. The experience of Helm in New York, Suppes in Stanford, and others who have worked on CAI with disadvantaged youth, would be invaluable here.

Of course, many other instructional problems in higher education lend themselves to technological analysis and solution. Course development and instructional design by teams of content specialists and behaviorally based media specialists will become a common pattern on campuses throughout the country. At Indiana, we now have a doctoral program in instructional development which prepares leaders of such teams. Their bases of operation will be in the offices of deans or directors of instruction on two- or four-year college campuses, or directors of instructional resources or learning resources in universities.

Bell also brings up the question of the rising cost of instruction. While not the main concern of this paper, the relationship between technology and teacher productivity should be commented upon. For a number of years we have been playing down, and even deprecating, the notion that considered use of technology with appropriate redeployment of staff and funds can reduce per pupil costs of instruction. However, certain forces operating at the present time will push us into a confrontation with the whole question of productivity. On the university level, Bell cites rising salaries and reduced teaching loads. At the same time taxpayers are resisting higher taxes to pay the increasing costs of higher education, students are militantly protesting fee or tuition raises.

While I am delivering this paper, students at Indiana University and Purdue are boycotting classes and preparing to march on the capital in one such protest. A few miles from where I stand, students of the University of Iowa are starting to organize a similar boycott. On the public school level, generally rising costs of education are causing taxpayer resistance, and the rate of turn-down on bond issues is becoming alarming. Teacher militancy is forcing the percentage of school funds assigned to salaries to a point where alternative means of handling instructional assignments are becoming more attractive to school boards. At the same time the professional loyalty that has kept administrators on the side of teachers on the question of technology and productivity is being eroded. Administrators are sure to take up, in the future, a position much more completely identified as management. As that takes place, administrators will feel freer to consider more efficient and more effective ways of deploying funds. That technology can increase instructional productivity I have no doubt, but the enabling structure of the educational enterprise will have to change drastically first (Heinich, 1969).

As I mentioned, the adolescent and postadolescent of today is accustomed to living in a constant bombardment of media, which give him the raw data he processes constantly. It is this constant access to source data which is unique in our age, giving each person a do-it-yourself kit in what's happening. It is a no-exit situation. Hayakawa postulated several years ago that television was responsible to a considerable extent for the current civil rights upheaval because it would not allow the black to escape into the ghetto. It followed him there, throwing up to him every evening the world he had no part of. Dick Gregory, in his prescient humor, once said it this way: "And when Dinah Shore blows that kiss out into the audience at the end of a show, you just know it's not for you."

Robert Heinich

The current anti-Vietnam war sentiment grew largely from having the war dumped daily into our living rooms—regardless of commentary, pro or con. It is an extremely existential situation, and raises the question as to what is the function of the academic when everyone has exposure to the data. Can he change his role from intermediary (between what occurs and his students) to co-discoverer and co-interpreter?

The student must stop having to shed the twentieth century when he enters a college classroom. The motion picture *is* slowly being accepted in academic circles. To be sure the majority of film showings on campus are arranged by film groups outside of class hours, but at least more and more films are being made accessible to students. The University of Southern California is the only institution, to my knowledge, that offers a credit course on the motion picture as part of the humanities sequence in the freshman year.

We ought also to create production teams skilled in mixed media to design presentations for those moments when key ideas need to be displayed in a fashion that affectively engages the student. Presentations shaped by perceptual and cognitive psychologies, again influenced by identification psychology, would help retain particularly those students who question the relevance of much of higher education.

But even more importantly, we must encourage, not simply allow, students to express themselves in nontraditional ways. The gates are coming down in regard to student expression in film; more and more universities and colleges are establishing programs in film production and expression. The best products from these schools are shown each year at Lincoln Center, as well as at many other festivals scattered around the country. Festivals of films made by high school students are now not unusual. All of this is tolerated, if not fully accepted, by the academic community.

This is all to the good. But there are newer media, such as light shows, electronic music with or without mixed media, and multi-image presentations that students are turning to in search of appropriate modes of expression. I just returned from the

161

annual convention of the Department of Audio-Visual Instruction of NEA where multi-image, mixed media presentations—mostly by students, and all with great impact—were playing to standing-room-only audiences. Showings of underground films at inconvenient hours were exceptionally well attended.

The students of the late James D. Finn paid tribute to him by means of a multi-image slide and film presentation that was far more deeply felt than anything they might have put to paper. There was no commentary as such. The still and motion images were all from Finn's life. The sound featured excerpts from the tribute delivered by Charles Hoban at the memorial service on April 5, excerpts from speeches by Finn, and a singularly appropriate song by Frank Sinatra, "My Way." The commentary the students made was in the way these raw data were assembled. This echoes my prior point that these newer means of expression are eliminating the expository, while putting each member of the audience in the position of inferring his own meaning and commentary, based on that part of the data relevant to him.

It is well worth noting that while great literature may not be written by committee, great presentations of this kind are. About six students put the Finn show together. The diverseness of the elements involved—the selection of slides, motion picture footage, graphics, audio excerpts, and music—and the complexities of the attendant editing jobs generate creative working arrangements with great inner flexibility, a very high tolerance for group effort, and a simultaneity of activity that is in striking contrast to the lineal working arrangement, garret and all, of the literary tradition. This should say something to us when we start work areas on campus.

Margaret Mead has commented that "young people are in modern times like native sons, whereas we others use the technology gingerly and talk like foreign born" (Goodman, 1969, p. 24). Most of us were raised in the old liberal arts tradition, which has had little to do with technology. In an article critical of the intellectual gloom with which that tradition tends to view technological developments, White (1966), a historian of technology, noted:

The new world in which we live is so unlike the past, even the past that is close to us, that in proportion that we are saturated in the Western cultural tradition we are incapacitated for looking clearly at our actual situation and thinking constructively about it. The better we are educated, the more we are fitted to live in a world that no longer exists [p. 224].

It is time to dispel the intellectual gloom in regard to technology in education and to make large-scale efforts to see what it might do for us. We may just find the new technology to be as great a boon to the scholar as the old technology of movable type. The first assistant professors born in the period after World War II will start teaching in a couple of years. We could just wait for them to start taking over. But I would hope we could do something more positive than simply fading away.

Commentary

Robert C. Snider

It is important for those of us in higher education to think very carefully about mechanization. Technology is fundamental to man's humanity. Civilization is built on the concept of man, the toolmaker. Bell defines *technology* as not simply a machine but a systematic disciplined approach to objectives. Technology is an unfortunate word in contemporary usage. Most people equate it with machines and actually it means systems or a systematic approach. Teaching and learning are basically different. Oliver Wendell Holmes, a hundred years ago, said that the stereopticon would be the great salvation for the schools. Fifty years later, at the turn of the century, Edison said the same thing about the motion

163

picture. Then, W. W. Charters said "radio," in 1932. Alvin Eunich in the early fifties said it would be television. But none of these things have been applied with enough attention to the symptoms ailing education, which, I think, are of basic concern here today. When they are better understood it will force a more systematic technology of instruction. One of the interesting things that the Commission on Instructional Technology learned during the last year is that institutions of higher education seem to have useful, promising, acceptable approaches to instructional technology, where the chancellor does not delegate to the faculty responsibilities for instruction, where the chancellor keeps instruction within his own area of responsibility.

O. W. Hascall

Our youngsters are well aware of technology. It is sad that they leave the technology behind when they enter the university campus.

Lee W. Cochran

The technological approach is not a matter of taking a key and unlocking technology or saying, "We are going to have technology." It is a matter of long strenuous training of a staff, especially for those who have never used technology in their teaching. Our College of Dentistry recently took a hard look at their own teaching-learning problems. Their extensive study includes putting dental subjects into a systems approach of learning, with computers and all different types of technological assistance such as films, slides, and materials of that nature. This was all done after a very thorough study based on six months of meetings, two hours a week, on studying technology. The group worked on computers, wrote programs for computers. From the very first meeting to the last meeting they had a seminar on this whole problem of how to approach learning by use of technology. The entire faculty was involved in deciding how they would approach instructional technology, making it acceptable and approved by all.

Robert Heinich

Our whole technology is changing and I think we are on the verge of one of the great developments of all time. We are going to see new methods of learning, new methods of course presentation. Technology is going to reduce some of the high educational costs that we have been encountering by placing responsibility on the individual learner, using machines and carefully prepared materials.

I would call your attention to several new technological developments. One is the new microfiche reader that may sell to students for about twenty-five dollars. A little four-by-six-inch card will have the contents of a 3,000-page book on it. The student can put it in his pocket and take it home and study. Second, the newly developed electronic-video recording equipment is going to lower the cost for mass distribution of pictoral material. It will greatly lower the cost of producing prints from an original video tape or film. A third recent development, one that is really going to take its place in education, is the cassette tape playback, which can be bought for twenty-five dollars. I think students are going to own their own microfiche book type reader, and their own cassette tape recorder or playback. A university can provide a cassette duplicating service which, for a very, very low cost, can duplicate programs. Students can take this to their own rooms, play it by use of an earphone, and not bother anybody. This kind of equipment can replace a great many of the large, expensive language laboratories in the very near future. Colleges could afford to buy a cassette playback for every student on the campus who would need it, for what we have invested in some of our language laboratories. Such developments are going to lower the price tag on education and make it possible to find ways to make technology work for the improvement of instruction.

Ralph W. Tyler

Academic Excellence
and
Equal Opportunity

Epilogue

Academic excellence and equal opportunity have no commonly accepted specific definitions. By *academic* I mean respects in which schools and colleges are expected to have special competence. When *excellence* is included with *academic,* I mean excellence in aims, in the degree to which aims are being reached, and in the efficiency of educational efforts. By *equal,* when applied to human beings, I mean that every individual is equally important as a person, is entitled to equal respect and to equal concern for his educational development. The issues about equality of opportunity are likely to focus on the wide differences in background, in interests, and in previous educational development of students and the implications of these differences for school and college policies and practices. My thesis is that educational institutions can effectively help in the education of a much larger proportion of youth than they are now reaching and at the same time increasing their academic excellence. I conclude that under current conditions, academic excellence and equal opportunity are compatible.

The recent widespread concern with civil rights has high-lighted the disparity in college enrollments of white middle-class students and youth from working-class families and from families with low incomes. Particularly evident is the smaller percentage of students from minority groups who are in our colleges and universities. The recognition of these widely different proportions of youth enrolled in post-high school educational institutions has stimulated efforts to open college doors more widely to so-called disadvantaged groups and to obtain greater financial support for their college attendance. It is clear that the use of the same admission standards and procedures for white middle-class applicants and for those from other backgrounds results in continuing disparity in proportions admitted even when the disadvantaged students are able to obtain increased financial support. This fact has engendered proposals to admit black students and others from minority groups without regard to admission standards. Some people have even proposed that those admitted from these backgrounds be assured that they would not be dropped from the college for failing their courses. The consideration of recommendations of this sort seems to pose a serious conflict between the use of higher institutions as means for redressing social injustices and inequalities and their employment as instruments for providing education of high quality. This apparent conflict gives rise to the subject of this chapter: Are academic excellence and equal opportunity compatible?

A thoughtful and comprehensive examination of this question to determine whether excellence and equality of opportunity are inherently in conflict or whether these two goals of a free society may be accommodated to each other, or even be complementary in their implementation, requires a critical review of several major factors. The first of these is the impact of the conditions on contemporary society and the social changes that can now be foreseen since education is an institution serving society and central to its development. Furthermore, educational opportunities for individuals are meaningless if those who are educated are not able to employ their talents in the society of which they are a part.

The establishment of colleges and universities took place before the industrial revolution and, of course, long before the emergence of our present, post-industrial society. When most people are unskilled laborers, only a few are needed for the occupational, social, and political elite. In the past, the schools have been more largely sorting and selecting agents than educational ones. Grades, examinations, and tests have been employed to sort people for courses, curricular tracks, admission to college, and the like. Although school officials and teachers have largely been unconscious of it, the curriculum itself—with its focus on middle-class illustrations, its assumptions regarding the backgrounds of children when they start to school, its pacing, its opportunities for pupil practice, and its reward system—has also been a major sorting instrument. This mechanism has been effective in limiting the number of "qualified" applicants for college to correspond roughly to the openings available to them on graduation in business, industrial, and political leadership, in the professions, and in the upper social strata. When I was in the elementary school more than half of my classmates dropped out before graduating from the eighth grade. They were able to get jobs on the farms and in other unskilled or semiskilled occupations. Only 10 per cent of my age mates graduated from high school, the others dropping out along the line to obtain employment or to help at home. Finally, only 3 per cent went on to college.

Now, however, in the contemporary, post-industrial society that characterizes the United States, only 5 per cent of the labor force is unskilled. Opportunities for employment in technical, professional, managerial, and service occupations have increased more than 300 per cent in one generation. While the uneducated and untrained comprise an alarming percentage of "hard core unemployed," demands are increasing for doctors, nurses, and health personnel generally, for teachers, supervisors, and others in education, for many kinds of workers in the social services and in the field of recreation, for accountants, administrators, engineers, and scientists. In civic life the need is great for citizens who are knowledgeable about our many serious domestic and international problems and who can examine alternative solutions objectively while strongly motivated by a keen sense of the public interest. As the importance of the family in a society where other primary institutions have lost much of their potency is being recognized, the need for parents who understand the functions of child rearing and are able to develop a strong setting for family members is increasingly expressed. Furthermore, the potential for individual self-realization offered by the variety of arts and indoor and outdoor recreational developments is now seen as heavily dependent upon an education that is humanistic in the best sense of the word. Our society is now seeking to identify potential talents of many sorts and to furnish opportunities for these talents to be actualized through education. Research on the brain and in behavioral genetics indicates that the learning requirements in our schools and colleges place no strain on the basic potential of the vast majority of human beings. Schools can be encouraged to help all students learn rather than to serve primarily as screening and sorting agencies.

This brief review of the developments in the larger society furnishes several facts relevant to our subject. The demand for college graduates is high and is continuing to increase. That a much greater number of students will make effective use of educational opportunities does not mean that many are doomed to failure to

169

find employment or to find other ways of utilizing their delevoped capacities constructively. This large expansion in the need for educated people has been accompanied by a great increase in the number and variety of abilities and skills demanded. Educational opportunities no longer must be limited to those with talents that fall within a relatively narrow range. Correspondingly, colleges and universities can broaden the range of student talents which they can help develop and the range of situations for which they prepare their graduates. We are coming nearer today than ever before to the old ideal of education for a free society, namely, aiding the student to gain an ever-widening range of alternatives in his life choices with each increment of education. Although ideal education has long been viewed as one in which the student is aided to find new doors of opportunity, in fact, in the past, many students have been trained ever more narrowly to fit into a niche in the economy. This condition is no longer justified. As far as our emerging post-industrial society is concerned, graduates in much larger numbers than before who have attained academic excellence will find expanding opportunities.

A second factor to be considered in our analysis of this subject is the extent to which a much larger percentage of youth are able to benefit from educational opportunities at the post-secondary level. This question is currently a source of great controversy and confusion. The question of inherent educational potential can never be answered in precise terms since inherent potential cannot be assessed directly. Evidence on this question is restricted to studies of biological, particularly neurological, structures and functions on the one hand and the outcome of educational efforts on the other. The confusion is also intensified by the failure to distinguish between questions that relate to the potential of an individual or a group of individuals to learn something and those that relate to the differential learning rates or outcomes among individuals or groups. That is to say, evidence that a given individual or group learns something more rapidly than others on the average, or in a given time attains a higher average level of performance than another individual or group, is often treated as though the evidence indicated that one individual or group could learn something and the other could not.

Learning is so characteristic of human individuals that one who fails to learn to acquire new patterns of behavior as he grows up is considered highly abnormal. From the standpoint of neural functioning, learning to use one's native language is about as demanding as any learning requirement of schools and colleges. To express an idea, one must draw upon extensive memory of words, must pattern the sentence structure in a way that is appropriate for the kind of meaning to be conveyed, and must utilize a particular appropriate inflection from a number of possibilities. Comprehension of what someone is saying is also complex in neurological functioning since the ambiguity of the alternative meanings of words and of sentence structures usually cannot be resolved until the entire sentence has been spoken. Since the vast majority of humans learn to use their native language, it appears probable that most human beings are inherently capable of learning complex behavior.

Another source of evidence is obtained from experiments in which efforts are made to teach deprived or otherwise handicapped individuals. The results are usually positive although the research reports often state that different individuals require different kinds of approaches to learning. Differences are also reported in the rates of learning and the accuracy of discrimination in transferring from the learning situation to other situations in which the learning could be applied.

It seems safe to conclude that we face no serious problem in finding many more youths who are capable of learning what colleges and universities seek to teach. In terms of human potential, academic excellence can be developed and maintained while at the same time the opportunities for higher education can be expanded to include a much larger proportion of youth than have been served in the past. But this conclusion immediately raises the question of the practicability of educating young people in college whose previous educational backgrounds have been inadequate. This question serves to focus on the real problems involved in seeking both to attain academic excellence and equality of opportunity. How far the problems are soluble depends to a major extent on the learning environment provided by the college.

For this reason, the third factor we need to examine in pursuing this subject is the effectiveness of the college learning environment. The essential conditions for learning in gross terms are indicated by the common description that it is a process in which one acquires new patterns of behavior, that is, new ways of thinking, feeling, and acting through practicing them. If the practice of the new behavior proves satisfying, it is continued until it becomes part of one's repertoire. Then it is said to have been learned. In these terms, the educational aims of colleges and universities are to aid students to learn what are believed to be important ways of thinking, feeling, and acting, ways of behaving that have not been part of the students' repertoires prior to their college attendance. When higher education is looked at in this way, academic excellence involves one or more of these three characteristics. It may be excellent because the ways of thinking, feeling, and acting that are being taught are of high importance to society and to the individual in contrast to patterns of behavior that have lesser value. It may be excellent because students develop a high level of competence in the new patterns of behavior. Or it may be excellent because the learning process itself is very efficient.

When equality of opportunity is viewed from the standpoint of learning, it involves one or more of these three characteristics. Every individual student will find opportunities to learn important ways of behaving that enable him to develop his talents in socially constructive and individually satisfying directions. Equality of opportunity may also mean that every individual student is aided to attain a high level of competence in the new patterns of behavior, or it may mean that the learning environment is so designed and the activities so directed that every student will be able to use his efforts efficiently in gaining his education.

Many current discussions assume the incompatibility in the college or university between these two sets of characteristics. Thus, it is often assumed that an institution of academic excellence will

172

set different educational objectives from one that seeks to provide opportunities for a large range of students. One set of objectives will emphasize the learning of principles, problem-solving, and creative composition with little or no reference to occupational relevance, while the objectives for the larger number of students will be the learning of facts, skills, conventional forms largely encompassed in an occupational area.

Furthermore, it is often assumed that the standards to be met in order to complete a course or program satisfactorily will represent different levels of competence, much higher levels for academic excellence than for the large majority of students. Finally, it is often assumed that an institution of academic excellence has much greater efficiency in its use of teaching and learning resources than one that serves a large majority of students. A review of studies that have been made of student learning in colleges and universities, or an extended observation on college campuses which includes interviews with faculty and students clearly reveals the questionable nature of these assumptions. Currently there is great confusion in all types of higher institutions regarding the educational objectives, standards of performance and what constitutes efficiency in learning. Clearing up some of this confusion might help in resolving the apparent conflict between excellence and equality of opportunity.

With reference to objectives, we should not lose sight of the fact that the case for college education rests on the fact that the various areas of scholarship provide resources upon which persons can draw in order to live more constructively, and with greater understanding and satisfaction. This expectation can be realized only if the student learns what kinds of contribution each subject area can provide, how to draw upon that area for its contributions, and how to use these contributions in dealing with the situations and problems he encounters from day to day. In the colleges, we have done little to identify concretely and in terms understandable to everyone the kinds of contributions to contemporary life that each subject area can provide. We have also done very little to help students learn how to draw on these contributions. We have tended to teach students what we think we know rather than how to carry on a life of continuing quest for understanding. We have been most remiss in failing to comprehend the concerns and situations of students who come from backgrounds different from our own. Hence, when they plead for relevance in what they are being taught, we know too little about the problems and situations that these students are encountering to help them see the way in which scholarship can contribute meaningfully to the effectiveness and satisfaction of their own lives. We are especially inclined to treat occupational concerns as unimportant, whereas for many youths the nature of one's occupation and his success in it are central to the quality of his life.

I believe that the result of our confusion over objectives is to limit greatly the number of students who perceive college education as anything more than a way of obtaining entry into a more prestigious, secure, or remunerative life. Without clarity as to what one is trying to learn, efforts are diffuse, unfocused, and relatively ineffectual. A small fraction of students discover for themselves, or have learned from a background where scholarship has been constructively utilized, what a good college education can be and they direct their efforts effectively. For them, one may speak of academic excellence but for many students neither excellence nor real educational opportunity is really provided.

Some understanding of this problem can be gained by considering more explicitly some of the conditions required for effective learning.

For one to acquire a relatively complex pattern of behavior, one has to have a clear notion of what he is trying to learn. If one has never seen a baseball game, he has great difficulty in learning if he is given only lectures on how to catch a ball. A student needs concrete examples of persons doing what he is expected to learn to do in order to guide his own efforts. These examples also help him judge the relevance and value to him of what he is learning. Unfortunately, many of our college students have never really observed someone using the fields of college scholarship as a resource for dealing with his own affairs. Instead, teachers lecture to him about specific topics that he does not perceive to have any clear relation to matters of importance to him. Hence, he tries to memo-

174

rize things he hears in lectures or reads in textbooks. Education would be better directed and more efficient if colleges gave conscious attention to the provision of models that would continually illustrate to students what style of life and what ways of behaving they are seeking to develop.

Astin's (1965) finding that the quality of a student's achievement in college is much more dependent upon the intellectual quality of other students than upon the quality of the faculty is probably a result of the failure of the faculty to provide learning models. The behavior of other students then becomes the guide to what one is to learn. The establishment of "learning communities" in our schools and colleges is thus essential to the development and maintenance of excellence and of wider educational opportunity. This affords a gross indication to students as to the nature of the learning they are being involved in.

A second major condition required for effective learning is motivation. Since a student must practice in order to learn something, his desire to learn it must be strong enough to impel him to an initial attempt and then to continue the practice. Strong motives for learning some particular behavior are commonly due to two factors. He is impelled to learn because he perceives the relevance of it to something important to him and he continues his learning efforts both because of the satisfaction he finds in learning and the value he discovers in what he has learned. The frequent complaint from many students today that their college work is irrelevant indicates that their motivation for classroom learning is low. Teachers can, of course, point out the connections between what they are teaching and the concerns that students have, but verbal explanations are less impressive than students' discovering relevance for themselves.

During 1958–60, an extensive investigation (Wilson and Lyons, 1961) was made of cooperative education-college programs, in which students alternate terms of full-time work with terms of full-time study. The report stressed the fact that both students and instructors found that the work experience helped students to understand the meaning of many of the things they were learning in college because they were able to use what they learned in their work, and their job activities raised questions which their studies helped them answer. This investigation also found that instructors of students who were in cooperative programs often sought to identify things they were teaching that had implications for the student's work and made a point of explaining the connection. Cooperative education is one important means for helping students to perceive the relevance of what they can learn in college, but there are other means as well, such as field work, community service activities, student tutoring programs. During the depression years the American Friends Service Committee operated summer programs for college students which involved them in work in the Appalachian highlands with the families of unemployed miners, helping in nutrition enrichment, the education and recreation of children, the building of community facilities. These activities were found to increase markedly the interest of students in learning when they saw how academic knowledge and skills could be used in these activities. Unfortunately, in many colleges, the opportunities to relate college courses to problems and interests of prime concern to students are not developed. Scholarship is treated as something that goes on in classrooms, libraries, and laboratories, isolated from the rest of life.

As students try to learn, seeking to practice the behavior they want to acquire, they need help in focusing their efforts on the significant features of the behavior. This is a third condition required for effective learning. Complex behavior, as in problem-solving, interpreting data, or writing an effective composition, involves a great many specific activities, many of which are relatively easy to acquire, but each of which has certain features that are crucial to satisfactory performance. The student needs to recognize these features and to be able to deal with them successfully. Expert coaches in the major sports have long recognized the value in helping players to focus their efforts at improvement on significant features. In many cases, motion pictures are taken of the behavior exhibited in football plays, swimming strokes, drives from the tee, and the like, and they are projected in slow motion to help the players identify crucial aspects and then to practice the effective ways of handling them. Of course, physical activities can be filmed because the behavior is largely visible. But intellectual and emotional behavior can also be analyzed, its aural and visual components can be recorded on motion picture film or video tape, and even without expensive recordings, instructors can themselves demonstrate these features or have outside experts do so, explaining verbally things that are not otherwise observable. Yet, this is rarely done in college classes. Instructors talk about what they have learned rather than showing students how to carry on inquiry. Teachers of composition commonly analyze the particular writing problem with which the students are dealing, pointing out features requiring special attention because of their difficulty and critical importance, but this kind of analysis is not common in most other college courses. Students flounder; some may quickly discover for themselves the significant features to which they must give attention and learn through trial and error how to deal with them, but many students never find out what the crucial factors are. Some years ago, Louis Gottschalk, professor of history at the University of Chicago, was impressed by the fact that most of his students were having great difficulty in trying to carry on historical inquiry. He realized that the lectures he had been giving explained what he had found through his own investigations but did not give any adequate description of the crucial aspects of the process of historical inquiry. He changed his lectures from reporting his findings to describing the significant features of his efforts to conduct historical studies. This proved to be much more helpful to students in attaining one objective of the course—to become able to conduct historical inquiry on questions relating to modern European history.

As we seek to aid all our students in learning, we shall need to provide in each subject help in focusing learning efforts on critical features of the behavior students are seeking to master.

A fourth essential condition for effective learning is ample opportunity for the practice of what is being learned in appropriate situations that are meaningful to the student. Students learn slowly if the only opportunities to practice are within the classroom. Contrast the rate at which one acquires a foreign language in the usual school situation with the rate when one is living in the country where he is continually called on to use the language. Furthermore, if he uses the language only in school, he quickly loses most of what he has learned when he is no longer in school. This is an illustration of the principle that efficient and effective learning requires immediate opportunities to practice and use the behavior acquired. Learning something now which cannot be practiced outside of the classroom until some distant future time is extremely ineffective as well as inefficient. For students who come from homes and communities where the conversation, activities, and concerns of many people are consistent with the behavior being learned in college, the opportunities to practice what they are learning are almost unlimited. For students from different environments, the college will need to help find opportunities for practice. In some cases, this may require changes in the curriculum so as to emphasize behavior clearly related to the concerns and activities of these students. In some cases, this may require explorations by students and faculty into the community outside to locate opportunities for practice that are now overlooked. In general this means a breaking down of the walls which isolate the college from the main currents of the lives of the students. As this is done, many situations will be found in the personal, social, political, economic environment as well as in the biophysical ecology of students such as in tutoring others, in social service enterprises, in full-time or part-time employment, in campus community projects. As students put to use outside the classroom what they are learning in college, they perceive its relevance more clearly and gain greater motivation for learning.

A fifth condition for effective learning is the provision of some means by which the learner can see how well he is performing and can identify the particular difficulties he is having in acquiring the new behavior. This specific feedback is necessary to develop greater competency or mastery than one displays on his initial efforts. Practice without information about specific inadequacies of one's behavior simply perpetuates those inadequacies.

One obvious factor that has greatly reduced the attention

we now give in college to providing specific feedback of this sort for our students is the large size of some classes. When I was in college, English Composition commonly enrolled less than twenty students per class. Each writing exercise we prepared was reviewed and criticized point by point by our instructors. Thus, we knew what weaknesses to work on as we prepared our subsequent assignments. This feedback was also provided us in other courses such as mathematics, science, economics. Now, with large enrollments, the older methods of review and criticism are no longer practicable. But specific feedback is still important, and new technology added to human ingenuity can do much more than most of us now do in furnishing our students with information to guide improved practice. For example, the invention of video tape machines and their lower price enable many teachers of courses in fields where the behavior to be learned can be analyzed by visual and oral records to use video tape as a means of specific feedback. At Stanford University students preparing to teach make video tapes of their teaching efforts, which are then reviewed and criticized by the student himself, by fellow students, and by teachers. Video tapes are being used in the education of nurses, physicians, psychologists, and anthropologists as well as teachers.

Other examples of technology in providing specific feedback are the use of sound recording in the teaching of foreign languages, the use of computers in recording and furnishing an analysis of steps the student follows in problem-solving, the use of the overhead projector to present to the entire composition class the review, criticism, and editing of typical student papers.

Examples of the use of ingenuity in devising ways of furnishing feedback are legion. Typically, they involve guides to student self-analysis, use of other students in criticism, reorganizing the instructor's use of time so as to provide time for analyzing student work. It thus appears possible for every student to get feedback in spite of large enrollments. This is especially needed by students who do not have in their homes or immediate neighborhood the opportunity for authentic, constructive criticism of their performance relating to the college objectives.

A sixth condition for effective learning is a reward system so that the students derive satisfaction from improved performance of the behavior they are learning. All of us realize that this reinforcement of desired behavior is basic to learning, and yet the reward systems in most colleges are very imperfect. Usually the grading system does not reward students in terms of what and how much they are learning, but merely for a high relative standing. Typically, the students who showed highest competence in the class at the beginning are the ones who show highest competence at the end of the course. They receive the high grades. Similarly, most of those who showed least competence at the beginning show least at the end. They receive low grades. Each group may have learned much or little, but the rewards received in terms of grades are not based on how much they have learned in the course. This obvious failure to establish a working system for rewarding learning could not be due to lack of ingenuity in devising such systems but rather from the failure to give attention to the problem.

Our own experience as adults in a program of learning something in which we are deeply interested will suggest the essential features of an effective reward system. Let us use as an example a program for learning to be a better golfer. We identify goals that seem important to us and attainable. In golf these might be to add to the length of our usual drive and to increase the accuracy of our putting on the green. Passing over the other steps in this program to the rewards, we recognize them in measurable progress toward our goals. When we find our average drives are fifty feet longer than they were previously, we are elated and keep practicing them. When we cut off an average of one stroke on the green we gain real satisfaction. Can we not devise reward systems in college that operate in a similar fashion?

Finally, I should like to mention a seventh condition that is essential for learning complex and difficult things—sequential organization of learning experiences. To attain a high level of understanding, of competence in inquiry, of skill in analysis and expression and of disciplined emotional response requires step by step development. Each new experience should build on previous

180

ones and go beyond them. Otherwise, the learner quickly reaches a plateau of mediocrity or lower. Unfortunately, the prevailing practice is to analyze courses and classify them primarily by content rather than by the increasing difficulty and complexity of the behavior to be learned. As a result we do not now have sound bases for organizing programs sequentially. Furthermore, the academic logrolling that is so prevalent in curriculum planning means either spreading courses around so that most of the students deal only with initial stages of learning in any one field or concentrating on specialization of content rather than orderly development of generalizable behavior. Thoughtful, deliberate, systematic attention to developing educational programs that insure opportunity for every student to learn sequentially should bring a payoff both in the effectiveness of learning and in the higher level of individual achievement.

I introduced these comments on conditions for effective learning to elaborate and illustrate the assertion that "For many students neither excellence nor real educational opportunity is usually provided." Real educational opportunity means that the conditions for effective learning are available to him. We know what some of these important conditions are but many students will not find them in their colleges. As a result, many students do not gain an excellent college education and many others gain their education quite inefficiently. The failure to provide essential conditions for learning is partly due to the fact that the typical college and university professor thinks of himself primarily as a scholar rather than as a teacher. Hence, he has not given the problem the serious study that would be expected if he viewed the learning of his students as his chief purpose. When we are ready to give our major attention to providing essential conditions of learning for all our students, we can begin to realize the possibility of increasing both academic excellence and equality of opportunity.

Thus far, I have dealt with the problem of compatibility largely in general or theoretical terms. In a particular college or university, however, the practical problem arises of using scarce resources wisely. Then, priorities need to be established because faculty time, facilities, and income are not unlimited. But within an individual institution the limits of resources available for the education of students can be greatly expanded by systematic attention to factors that now are overlooked, or given only a cursory glance. The college needs to identify more clearly and selectively what important objectives it should be striving to attain. It should study the conditions essential for its students to learn and see that they are provided. The college must open its doors to the wider community so that its curriculum can have contemporary meaning, its students will be able to practice and use what they are learning, and it can have the benefit of additional resources for learning provided by children, youth, and adults outside the college. The college emphasis will need to be on the student learning to manipulate his total environment for his own educational development. In this kind of atmosphere, it is easier for students to discover constraints that are not arbitrary impositions of authority but naturally inhere in the situation, and also easier to come to terms with these constraints in some cases by accepting them and in others by overcoming them because he sees that they lie within situations that he can understand. In general, opening the college to the large society aids the student in keeping contact with reality rather than feeling that he is in a hothouse where the conditions are all set and controlled by the faculty and administration. This openness should be accompanied by increasing opportunities for him to manipulate his environment both within and without the college since this is so essential for responsible adulthood.

The educational program both for academic excellence and for equality of opportunity is an open-ended one, that is, one that is never finished and is always capable of redirection. It involves the building of solid foundations of learning, and the step-by-step development of greater understanding, broader and deeper interests, increased competence in study, analysis, and problem-solving, ever-increasing receptivity to esthetic experience, and human relationships accompanied by ever-more-meaningful responses. If we can help each student build a solid foundation and keep on learning for each step of his development, the college is not setting either unattainably high standards or shoddy low ones, but it is enabling each student to set standards for his college work that represent solid educational attainment. The conclusion that I am drawing from this review of the contemporary situation in American higher education is that educational institutions can effectively help in the education of a much larger proportion of youth than is now being reached while at the same time their academic excellence can be greatly increased.

Bibliography

ASTIN, A. W. *Who Goes Where to College?* Chicago: Science Research Associates, 1965.

BELL, D. *The Reforming of General Education: The Columbia College Experience in Its National Setting.* New York: Columbia University Press, 1966.

CAMPBELL, D. P. "The Vocational Interests of Dartmouth College Freshmen: 1947–67." *Personnel and Guidance Journal,* 1969, *47*(6), 521–530.

Carnegie Commission on Higher Education. *Quality and Equality: New Levels of Federal Responsibility for Higher Education.* A Special Report of the Commission, December 1968.

COHN-BENDIT, D., AND COHN-BENDIT, G. *Obsolete Communism: The Left-wing Alternative.* New York: McGraw-Hill, 1969.

COLEMAN, J. S., *et al. Equality of Educational Opportunity.* Washington, D.C.: U.S. Office of Education, 1966.

Department of Health, Education, and Welfare. *Toward a Long-Range Plan for Federal Financial Support for Higher Education.* Report to the President, January 1969.

DRUCKER, P. F. *The Age of Discontinuity: Guidelines to Our Changing Society.* New York: Harper, 1968.

185

DUBOIS, W. E. B. *The Souls of Black Folk*. Greenwich, Conn.: Fawcett, 1961.

FELDMAN, K. A., AND NEWCOMB, T. M. *The Impact of College on Students*. San Francisco: Jossey-Bass, 1969.

FISCHER, J. "The Case for the Rebellious Students and Their Counterrevolution." *Harper's*, August, 1968.

GOODMAN, P. "The Present Moment in Education." *The New York Review of Books*, April 10, 1969.

GORDON, K. (Ed.). *Agenda for the Nation*. Washington, D.C.: The Brookings Institution, 1968.

Harvard Committee. *General Education in a Free Society*. Cambridge: Harvard University Press, 1945.

HEINICH, R. "Technology of Instruction: Impetus and Impasse." In E. L. Morphet and D. L. Jesser (Eds.), *Planning for Effective Utilization of Technology in Education*. New York: Citation Press, 1969.

HEIST, P. "Creative Students—College Transients." In P. Heist (Ed.), *The Creative College Student: An Unmet Challenge*. San Francisco: Jossey-Bass, 1968.

JACKSON, P. W. *The Teacher and the Machine*. Pittsburgh: The University of Pittsburgh Press, 1968.

KUNEN, J. S. *The Strawberry Statement: Notes of a College Revolutionary*. New York: Random, 1969.

LERNER, M. *America as a Civilization*. New York: Simon and Schuster, 1957.

LERNER, M. "The Negro American and His City: Person in Place in Culture." *Daedalus*, Fall 1968, *97*, 1390–1408.

LEWIS, O. *La Vida: A Puerto Rican Family in the Culture of Poverty, San Juan and New York*. New York: Random, 1966.

MACKINNON, D. W. "The Nature and Nurture of Creative Talent." *American Psychologist*, 1962, *17*, 484–485.

MOYNIHAN, D. P. "The Impact on Manpower Development and Employment of Youth." In E. J. McGrath (Ed.), *Universal Higher Education*. New York: McGraw-Hill, 1966.

PEARSON, R. "Admission to College." In E. J. McGrath (Ed.), *Universal Higher Education*. New York: McGraw-Hill, 1966.

ROMULO, C. Address. In United Nations General Assembly, *Official Records*, Twenty-third Session, 1968. Plenary, 1736.

SCHAGRIN, M. L. Letter to *Science*, April 1969, 245.

SCHWAB, J. J. *College Curriculum and Student Protest*. Chicago: The University of Chicago Press, 1969.

Bibliography

TRENT, J. W., AND MEDSKER, L. L. *Beyond High School.* San Francisco: Jossey-Bass, 1968.

WHITE, L., JR. "On Intellectual Gloom." *The American Scholar,* Spring 1966, *35*(2), 223–226.

WILSON, J. W., AND LYONS, E. H. *Work-Study College Programs.* New York: Harper, 1961.

Index

Index

C

CAMPBELL, D. P., 6, 85–97
Carnegie Commission on Higher Education, 52
Changes: and erosion of belief, 30; and revolution, 28, 29
Chicago, 26–27, 43; Democratic Convention of, 26–27; University of, 43
Cities, crisis in, 4. *See also* Ghettos, inner-city
Civil rights, 3
Cluster colleges, 51
COCHRAN, L. W., 164
COFFELT, J. J., 151
COHN-BENDIT, D., 118, 125
COLE, N. S., 137
COLEMAN, J. S., 59
College management: budget of, 7; operating systems of, 7
Columbia University, 24, 26, 40, 43, 113, 124, 132
Communication: among students, 115; and guidance, 106; to solve problems of universities, 139; with students, 38, 39; those involved with, 66
Conferences, 103
Constitution of the United States, 20
Cornell University, 40, 120, 121, 122, 136
CROCKETT, D. S., 24
Curriculum: for disadvantaged, 49; and faculty, 79, 116; in Negro colleges, 104; reform of, 118; required, 80; students and, 6

D

Dartmouth College, admissions at, 88, 89
Declaration of Independence, 21, 35
Department of Health, Education, and Welfare, 53
Disadvantaged: definition of, 48; education for, 49

Drop-outs, 62–64, 101
DRUCKER, P. F., 29
DUBOIS, W. E. B., 18–19
DUGAN, W. E., 5, 45–55

E

EDMISON, L. D., 68
Education, 45, 46; conferences about, 103; and learning environment, 172; opportunities for, 170; and potential, 170–171; and social changes, 8. *See also* Higher education; Vocational-technical education
Elementary and Secondary Education Act, 48
Equal opportunity, 3; and academic excellence, 8, 166–183; for all, 14, 45; and competence, 172; to education, 46, 55; to higher education, 5. *See also* Access; Opportunity; Education; Academic excellence
EWIGLEBEN, R. L., 138

F

Faculty: and admissions, 87; and campus problems, 8; and curricula, 6, 79, 116; and educational theory, 79; and governance, 78; interest of in teaching, 64; power of, 6; restraint of, 78; uninterested, 119, 120; and university organizational structure, 143
Federalist Papers, 20–22
FELDMAN, K. A., 90
Financial aid to college students: funds for, 54; program for, 55
FINN, J. D., 162
FISCHER, J., 132

G

GARDNER, J., 92
Ghettos, inner-city, 30; and American dream, 30; culture of, 33; of

Index

New York, 33; population of, 32; and revolution, 31. *See also* Cities, crisis in

G. I. Bill, 47

GOODMAN, P., 157, 162

GORDON, K., 3

GOTTSCHALK, L., 177

Governance: of college campus, 6, 7, 77, 78; student participation in, 135

Grading system, 75; and evaluation of progress, 81; pass-fail, 78

Guidance: and communication, 106; and relevance, 99–107; services, 6, 7; theory and practice of, 103

H

HAMILTON, A., 21

HARCLEROAD, F. F., 1–9

Harvard, 24, 94, 120, 126, 132, 134, 136

HASCALL, O. W., 164

Head Start, 50, 155

Health, Education, and Welfare, Department of, 53, 54

HEINICH, R., 7, 8, 154–165

HEINY, L., 82

HEIST, P., 62

Higher education, access to, 5, 46; and educational objectives, 173; failures in, 64; and learning, 172; organization in, 143; planning in, 151–152; provision for, 5; students in, 47; troubles in, 71–72. *See also* Universities; Institutions of higher education

Higher Education Act, 47, 48

HOYT, D. P., 68

HUBBARD, P. G., 152

I

Institutions of higher education: credibility of, 4; location of, 3; number of, 2; students in, 2

J

JACKSON, P. W., 157

JAMES, W., 62, 63

JEFFERSON, T., 14, 30

Junior colleges, growth of, 51

K

KUNEN, J., 113, 119, 127

L

LASKI, H., 30

LAWRENCE, P. F., 24

Learning, 171–181; and environment, 172, 182; motivation for, 175; from peers, 175; and reward, 180; and technology, 179

LERNER, M., 4, 26–44

LEWIS, O., 32–33

LYONS, E. H., 175

M

MC CAIN, J. A., 131–139

MAC KINNON, D. W., 63

Management, college, 140–151; budgeting in, 147–148; and continuing change, 146; and faculty, 143, 144; and management information system, 149–150; and role of administration, 142; techniques of, 142

MEAD, M., 162

MEDSKER, L. L., 54

Minorities: guidance for, 7; T.V. impact on, 4

MOYNIHAN, D. P., 59

MUNDAY, L. A., 54

N

National Defense Education Act, 47

National Student Association, 6, 73

Negroes, American, 18–19; admissions of in Illinois, 95; colleges and curriculum for, 104; in ghetto, 33; and revolution, 39; wants of, 32

Index

NELSON, T. M., 6, 98–107
NEWCOMB, T. M., 90

O

Opportunity, 45–55; and academic excellence, 166–183; educational, 46, 55. *See also* Access; Equal opportunity
OSTAR, A. W., 5, 54

P

Pass-fail, 78
PEARSON, R., 59
Permissiveness: of American family, 42; in universities, 73
POWELL, R. S., JR., 6, 71–84
Priorities, 14–17, 20, 21, 24; and college testing, 16; of educational values, 16; of order, 14; of peace, 14; who determines, 24
Protest movement, and American students, 115. *See also* Violence; Revolution

R

Research, local, campus, 102
Revolution: and black community, 119; changes, short of, 28, 29; groups interested in, 39; inner-city, 30, 34; minorities and, 39; and world student movement, 113
RIESMAN, D., 42
ROBINSON, D. D., 7, 140–153
ROBINSON, T. R., 97
ROMULO, C., 115, 116

S

SALINGER, J. D., 109–110
San Francisco State, 121, 123
SANFORD, N., 5, 56–68
SCHAGRIN, M. L., 87
SCHELER, M., 31
SCHWAB, J. J., 156
SEXTON, T. G., 95

SMITH, A. E., 84
SNIDER, R. C., 163
SOSKIN, W., 66
Strong Vocational Interest Blank (SVIB), 89
Student unrest, 7, 24, 108–128, 131–139; coping with, 134–135, 137; reasons for, 7, 24. *See also* Violence
Students: and curricula, 6, 135; on moral issues, 125; in the 1930s, 37; in policy formation, 135, 139; power of, 73

T

Talent, 57–68; defined, 60; development of, 59; of individual, 57; loss of, 61, 63; shortage of, 65
TAYLOR, H., 3, 6, 108–128
Teaching, 8; changes in, 68
Technology, 154–165, 179; and Computer Administered Instruction (CAI), 159; definition of, 163; and mechanization, 157; new developments, 165; problems of, 7; and protest, 8; and remedial programs, 158–159; results of, 8; and students, 7, 155–157, 161; and teacher productivity, 159; technicians for, 57; training for, 164; use on campus, 155
Television: impact of, 4; and inner-city ghetto, 33, 34
Testing, 99–102; and ACT, 101–102; history of, 99; relevance of, 100; tools of, 101–102. *See also* Assessment instruments
THOMPSON, R. B., 138–139
TRENT, J. W., 54
Tuition, 5
TYLER, R., 8, 166–183

U

Undergraduate institutions, diversity in, 5

Index

Universities: defined, 13; management of, 140–151; new courses in, 23; for nonviolent education, 124; as political institutions, 76; relating to the community, 138; urban, 51, 76

University of California, Berkeley, 66, 132; free speech movement in, 81, 112

Upward Bound, 50

Urban crisis, 26–43

V

VARNER, C., 83

Vietnam, peace in, 14

Violence: in American society, 41; and change, 6, 83; controlling, 124; and discussion, 83; exclusion of, 22; and radical student movement, 117; results of, 7; short of revolution, 22; at University of Paris, 132. *See also* Student unrest

Vocational-Technical Education expanding, 52. *See also* Education; Vocational-Technical Education Act

Vocational-Technical Education Act, 47

W

West Point, 90–91

WHITE, L., JR., 162

WIEMANN, C. B., JR., 106

WILSON, J. W., 175

WILSON, O. M., 4, 13–25

WRENN, C. G., 101

Y

Yale, 92